Life is a Game!

Keys for a light and purposeful life full of Joy

Life is a Game!

Jan Vermeiren

Life is a Game: www.life-is-a-game.org

Cover: Graffito

Artwork: Priscilla Peeters

Legal depot: D/2014/13.543/2

CIP Koninklijke Bibliotheek Albert I

NUR: 734, 728

Contents

Introduction

Why this book?

After creating a company (Step by Step Consulting, which became more known under the brand name Networking Coach) and writing a few books (of which two, *Let's Connect!* and *How to REALLY use LinkedIn* were international best sellers), I found myself in a kind of burnout. I explicitly write 'a kind of burnout', because it didn't shut me down completely like burnouts do many other people. What did happen, however, was that I almost lost my joy of life.

I had lots of success in the business world, but what was that actually about? What is success, really? I discovered that I was most focused on wanting to be accepted by the outside world. I was ready to defend myself against anyone who had the smallest amount of criticism about me or my work. This is just one 'flavor' of the many ways that people make their lives harder than they need to.

"How could this happen to me?" I thought. "I, who have been on the path of personal and spiritual growth for so many years, should know better. This success path is the foundation of my first two books. I should know the solution." But I didn't. At least, I did not know it until I was ready to go beyond everything I knew, not until I was ready to embrace a whole new perspective on life. I attained a whole new perspective on what I now call 'the human game'.

With that new perspective, everything quickly started to change. I felt better and much lighter. I had fewer problems. The problems I did have were smaller... or I was able to deal with them better, faster, more easily. It was then that I began to understand the real meaning of the word 'en-lighten-ment'. I realized that it is not about becoming so 'spiritual' that the body suddenly disappears and the mind becomes one with God, or something like that (which seems like an unattainable goal anyway). No, it is about living my life as a human being and becoming 'lighter' while still being in the body. In other words: having less sorrow and conflict and more joy and happiness!

I also discovered that there are three phases in the human game. I discovered that the first phase indeed contains experiencing pain, fear, and rejection, and that it is part of the plan/game. Without it we can't go to phases two and three.

In this book I'm sharing my insights and experiences about playing the human game and how to go from phase one to phase two... and finally on to phase three. I'm using several simple analogies for this process. My insights and experiences include analogies with monsters, teddy bears, robots, trains, radio stations, GPS systems, and even computer games (which may be surprising at first, but you will find out how much sense they make and how much more 'light and air' is infused into the human game by using them).

I'm also sharing the fears I had before and during the creation of this book. It was scary, very scary, at first, but the process helped me to become lighter and to experience fully everything that I'm sharing in this book. Although my life is not your life, I hope that my personal experiences (both the 'good' and the 'bad') inspire you.

The purpose of this book is to provide you with insights and practical tips to move out of the 'Fearful Game of Life' into the 'Joyful Game of Life'.

In other words, the book is about finding the natural state of joy again. It includes:

1. Understanding what the human game is about, and the phases of the game.
2. How to loosen resistance to the 'bad stuff' that may seem to happen to you, and as a consequence feel lighter.
3. How to connect to the natural state of joy that is inside and outside of us all the time.

As a fellow player of the Game of Life, I greet you with much love!

Jan

Chapter 1: The Game

Many people wonder about the meaning of life. They ask themselves, "What am I doing here?" They may even think, "I feel like a stranger on this planet."

Since my teenage years, I have had thoughts and feelings like these myself. Like most teenagers, my search was more about how to fit into this world than to make sense of it all, although those seeds were already there. My true 'spiritual search' began later on, in my mid-twenties. Now that I'm almost 40, I think I have found what life is all about. I write 'think' because I have had many moments in my life where I thought, "This is it!" — only to gain new insights later, or to feel sometime after that something was missing. In other words, this book comprises my findings to this moment. I assume that as long as I'm here on this planet, I will remain a student of life. There will always will be new things to discover and new questions to answer.

The good news is that now I have found a kind of peace from within. It is from this place that I am studying (as opposed to the restless 'hunt for more' I experienced before). My intention with this book is to share how I found this peace. I hope to inspire you to find it as well... and to help you go beyond it in your life.

The problem with many of the spiritual teachings I studied was that the language was old-fashioned or the concepts were too abstract. This is why I changed them. As soon as I started to explain the insights I had received using analogies, metaphors, and examples from my own life, others started to grasp them too. That inspired me to look at which analogies work best. What I found is that using computer games to explain how life works actually does the job pretty well. I will use many other analogies and examples in the book, like trains, GPS systems, radio stations, monsters, and teddy bears, but let's start with the computer game.

The Computer Game

Games that are played over the Internet are very popular. Many players have access to them. One of the most popular and most played games worldwide is *League Of Legends* (**www.leagueoflegends.com**). According to Wikipedia, as of January 2014, "over 67 million people play *League of Legends* per month, 27 million per day, and over 7.5 million concurrently during peak hours."

As this game is so popular, let's use it to make an analogy.

Note: If you have never played a computer or video game, or don't understand everything I share on the next pages, relax. Computer games are just one of the analogies I'm using in this book. Even without the computer game analogies, the rest of the book is easy to understand.

In short, the game of *League of Legends* is about two teams who try to capture each other's fortress. Each team consists of 1, 3, or 5 players, depending on the game mode.

In every game, each player chooses a character. This character is called a 'champion'. Each champion has its own characteristics, its own pros and cons or strengths and weaknesses. Think of champions as superheroes, each with their specific abilities and skills. People tend to have more of an affinity for some champions than others. Certain champions have the skill set that more closely fits the way the player wants to play the game. It's just a personal preference. In the same way that some people might prefer Superman over Batman or Spiderman, some people prefer one champion over another.

There are several game modes, but the bottom-line is that it allows you to play against a friend (or a stranger) in one game and then play alongside the same person in the next game. Are you beginning to see why I selected this game as an analogy for life?

Let's begin by looking at the screen that you see when you play the game. I will first explain what you will see. You can then look at the image below to see how it actually appears. This gives you an image in your mind, then a true visual to which you can compare it.

When actually playing the game, you'll see a small part of the map in what is called a bird's eye view (as seen from above). What your **champion** will interact with directly is seen in the middle of the screen. However, as a **player** you also have an overview, which is the 'mini map' on the right hand side, at the bottom of your screen. This is where you have an overview of the whole area, including a view of your teammates and your adversaries. The white box on the mini map is what you see enlarged in the middle of your screen.

| Teammates | Other team | White box: Part of Mini Map that you see in full screen in front of you | Mini Map with allied fort bottom left corner and adversaries' fort top right |

In other words, as a player your Mini Map provides you with an overview of the game. The champion only has a limited view. However, there is still a part of the map that is black when you, as a player, look at it. In the game this is called the 'fog of war' (refer to the image on the following page). When there are no allied troops in a particular part of the map, the 'fog of war' is in place and you can't see what is happening there. So, sometimes you don't see the adversaries on the Mini Map because there are no allied troops near them. However, you still know that they are somewhere out there, because the number of allies and adversaries is always the same. That's how the game is designed.

The game also offers a chat function so players from the same team can communicate with each other (refer to the image on the following page). This enables them to work together, ask for help, or alert teammates.

Chat function

Fog of war (black area)

Fog of war (black area)

Now, in order to play the game, you need to give your champion orders. Your champion doesn't move or do anything proactively. The only thing it can do by itself is react: it defends itself when it is attacked. For your champion to take action, you need to do something. You do this by moving and clicking your mouse and tapping a few keys on the keyboard. In this way, your champion can attack the other team, use an ability, or heal an allied champion. In other words, the champion needs input to initiate action.

In the game, your champion has a health bar, which tells you how much health that champion has left. This gives you the data you need to decide whether to move more toward the other team, risking some of your health, or to retreat and protect your health. This feedback is crucial for making decisions that will allow you to remain in the game. Whenever your champion gets hit, it affects the champion's health bar negatively, but you may still play. Your champion doesn't feel physical pain. Even when a champion dies, nothing emotional, painful, or otherwise bad happens to it. You just have to wait for a while for your champion to come back so you can continue to play. It resurrects, so to speak.

To sum it up:

1. You need a character, a champion to play. Otherwise you only can watch (which may be fun once in a while, but doesn't give you the same satisfaction, joy, and excitement you get by playing yourself).
2. You have the overview, but the champion doesn't.
3. The champion needs input in order to move. In its basic position, the champion is only reactive: it retaliates in response to attacks from the other team. When it gets input from the player, it can initiate action.
4. You need feedback from the champion in order to keep it safe and to think about new or alternative strategies.
5. You can communicate with the other players via the chat function to discuss strategies from a bird's eye view. Champions only attack or defend against the champions from the other team; they can heal the champions of their teammates.
6. Although there are some blind spots (fog of war), you know the necessary elements (adversaries) are there so you can play the game and enjoy the experience. You don't question it; you are sure of it because that's how the game is designed.
7. In one game you are competing against a friend, while in the next game that friend can be your teammate. Both can provide equal fun!
8. You will have a greater affinity for some champions compared to others. One is not better than the other, but some are better for your experience, approach, and personal skills. Other players may have other preferences, but the good part is, everyone has a champion with which they can identify.
9. The champions don't experience pain when they are hit or die. At least, that is the experience of the player.
10. Although there is lots of fighting going on, in the end, it is just a way to have an experience you can't have as a human being. It is only a game.

The Human Game

Now that we have laid the foundation regarding the computer game, let's look at life as a human being. I will come back to the computer game shortly so you will understand why I'm making the analogy.

How do people look at their lives? You'll probably recognize one or more of these points of view in your own life, or in the lives of people around you:

- I'm stuck in this body. There are some pros, but I'm more focused on the cons.
- I'm struggling to survive.
- I have the feeling that I constantly have to defend myself. Other people (boss, colleagues, parents, siblings) are always out to attack, upset, or derail me.
- I'm sometimes very happy and most of the time I'm content. So, I can't complain, but I also feel that I'm missing something. I feel there is something more I should/can be doing here, but I don't have a clue about what it is or where to look for it.
- What is the meaning of all of this? What is the meaning of life? Why am I here?

Although I can't give you the definitive answer to the last question (but I will share my view later on in the book), it's interesting to see that these questions share some similarities with a computer game.

Of course, every analogy or metaphor has its limits and limitations, but I have found that computer games may reveal some of the answers for becoming en-light-ened. I'm not talking about the clichéd 'monk on a mountaintop all day long' who, at some point, is so full of light he disappears into star dust. What I mean by finding 'answers to get en-light-ened' is finding some insights and ways to make our human lives a lot lighter, easier, and more effortless. That is, we experience more happiness, love, and joy. And then, well, who knows what may happen next?

So let's look at the analogy. Let's start with mapping out the computer game as the game we play as humans, also called life ☺.

Let's assume that the character or champion is you (or me) in our human form and that the player is our Higher Self, Inner Being, Soul, Spirit or whatever name you use for the connection with the Source or God. Once we have this, then we have a nice model to work with. For the sake of keeping things simple, let's use the words 'Human Form' and 'Higher Self'.

Now, let's review our summary of the computer game and replace it with the words of the human game. In other words, we replace the word 'champion' with 'Human Form' and the word 'player' with 'Higher Self'.

1. Your Higher Self needs a Human Form to play. Otherwise It only can watch. Watching may be fun once in a while, but doesn't give the same satisfaction, joy, and excitement than playing.
2. Your Higher Self has the overview; your Human Form doesn't.
3. Your Human Form needs input in order to move. In its basic position, the Human Form is only able to be reactive. It retaliates or only responds to attacks from the other team. When it gets input from the Higher Self, it can take action.
4. Your Higher Self needs feedback from your Human Form in order to keep the Human Form safe and to think about new or alternative strategies.
5. Your Higher Self can communicate with other Higher Selves to discuss strategies from a helicopter view. The Human Forms only attack/defend the Human Forms from the 'other' team and can heal the Human Forms of their 'own' team.
6. Although there are some blind spots, your Higher Self knows the necessary elements are there so It can play the game and enjoy the experience. Your Higher Self doesn't question it. It is sure of it, because that's how the game is designed.
7. In one game your Higher Self is competing against a friend, while in the next game that friend can be Its teammate. Both can provide equal fun!
8. With some Human Forms (in this case: bodies) your Higher Self has a better affinity than with others. One is not better than the other, but they are more suited for your experience, while other Higher Selves have other preferences.
9. The Human Forms don't experience pain when they are hit or die or, at least, that is the experience of the Higher Self.
10. Although there is lots of fighting going on, in the end it is simply a way to have an experience your Higher Self can't have as a non-physical being. It is just a game.

Interesting, right? ☺

Now, let's look more in detail at the 10 elements and see how they play out in our daily lives.

Your Higher Self needs a Human Form to play. Otherwise It only can watch. Watching may be fun once in a while, but it doesn't give the satisfaction, joy and excitement than playing.

What does this mean?

First, it means your Human Form is part of a bigger You. Second, it means your Human Form is a form that your Higher Self **needs** to have certain experiences. In its non-physical state, it cannot smell the sweet scent of flowers, see a beautiful sunrise, taste delicious meals, hear the joyful singing of birds, or feel the gentle touch of a fellow human being. If there was no Human Form, your Higher Self would never know what being human would be like. It would miss out on experiences that It desires for Its own joy.

It is similar to playing computer games: you can have the experience of being a hobbit, a racecar driver, or a superhero. Although you are not a hobbit, a racecar driver, or a superhero, a computer game allows you to have an experience that simulates being those things. Yes, it's fun to watch someone else play a computer game once in a while, especially when we're trying to learn the game ourselves. However, it is always much more fun to play the game ourselves. Even if we are not as good as the person we're watching, there's just something more fun about getting involved personally and playing the game ourselves.

Your Higher Self has the overview, your Human Form hasn't.

How many times have you experienced luck, synchronicity, or serendipity? How many times have you said: "Wow, I can't believe this has happened! What are the odds? This is sheer luck!"

But is it?

Let's look at our computer game analogy again.

In the computer game, the champion doesn't know where the other team members are, but the player does. He has the overview. He sees them on the mini map. From this overview the player can guide the champion to the place it needs to be. The same applies in our daily lives. Our Higher Self has that grand overview that we don't. Our Higher Self constantly guides us. Most of us haven't realized that yet. Sometimes we do something and when others ask, "Why did you do that?" the only answer we can give is, "It was a gut feeling," or "I followed my intuition."

What actually happened?

16

In those intuitive moments, our Higher Self guided us. It nudged us in the right direction. It whispered some ideas in our ears, planted a solution in our minds …

The example above was rather 'positive'. However, sometimes it also happens in a way we perceive as 'negative'.

We may tell ourselves, "I listened to my intuition and now I have broken my leg. I don't like it. I'm not going to trust that guidance again." That's one of the reasons why people seem to lose their connection to their Higher Self. (Actually you can't lose the connection; it is always there. But you can choose to listen or not.)

Now, anytime you *really* listen to your intuition — to your Higher Self — it is always for the better. The problem is, you can't see the bigger picture. You perceive events as good or bad, as positive or negative. But because you don't have the overview, you never know if that actually is the case! Sometimes you just need to take it on faith that your Higher Power is doing the right thing from its perspective, not yours. Maybe being fired has a more positive meaning in the bigger picture, although in the short term there may be some drama and financial distress involved. Losing one job or advantage may feel like a devastating loss in the moment, but that loss also makes room for new opportunities (at least that's what happened early on in my career ☺).

Let me share the Story of the Farmer's Son with you to give you another example.

> *One day in late summer, an old farmer was working in his field with his old sick horse. The farmer felt compassion for the horse and desired to lift its burden. So he let his horse loose to go to the mountains and live out the rest of its life.*
>
> *Soon after, neighbors from the nearby village visited, offering their condolences, and said, "What a shame. Now your only horse is gone. How unfortunate you are! You must be very sad. How will you live, work the land, and prosper?" The farmer replied, "Who knows? We shall see."*
>
> *Two days later the old horse came back, rejuvenated after meandering on the mountainsides while eating the wild grasses. He came back with twelve younger, healthier horses that followed the old horse into the corral.*
>
> *Word got out in the village of the old farmer's good fortune and it wasn't long before people stopped by to congratulate the farmer on his good luck. "How fortunate you are!" they exclaimed. You must be very happy!" Again, the farmer said, "Who knows? We shall see."*

At daybreak on the next morning, the farmer's only son set off to attempt to train the new wild horses, but was thrown to the ground and broke his leg. One by one villagers arrived during the day to bemoan the farmer's latest misfortune. "Oh, what a tragedy! Your son won't be able to help you farm with a broken leg. You'll have to do all the work yourself. How will you survive? You must be very sad," they said. Calmly going about his usual business, the farmer answered, "Who knows? We shall see."

Several days later a war broke out. The Emperor's men arrived in the village demanding that the young men come with them to be conscripted into the Emperor's army. As it happened, the farmer's son was deemed unfit to serve the Emperor because of his broken leg. "What very good fortune you have!!" the villagers exclaimed as their own young sons were marched away to battle. "You must be very happy." "Who knows? We shall see," replied the old farmer as he headed off to work his field alone.

As time went on, the broken leg healed, but the son was left with a slight limp. Again the neighbors came to pay their condolences. "Oh what bad luck," they said. "Too bad for you!" But the old farmer simply replied, "Who knows? We shall see."

As it turned out, the other young village boys all died in the war, and the old farmer and his son were the only able bodied men capable of working the village lands. The old farmer became wealthy and was very generous to the villagers. They said, "Oh how fortunate we are. You must be very happy." To this, the old farmer replied, "Who knows? We shall see!"

Is something good or is it bad? Who knows? In our Human Forms, we don't see the bigger picture. But when we are aligned with our Higher Selves, we will get the right circumstances and ingredients to play our game. From the helicopter's view, our Higher Selves can guide us towards the experiences we desire.

Your Human Form needs input in order to move. In its basic position, the Human Form is only reactive. It can only respond or retaliate in response to attacks from the other team. However, when it gets input from the Higher Self, it can take thoughtful, directed action.

We are constantly receiving input from our Higher Selves, but most of the time we are not aware of it. It's as though the sound and audiovisual information is there, but the speakers and the monitors are turned down or off. The only reason we don't hear or see the information streaming into our lives 24/7 is that most of us haven't cultivated the ability (or practiced the art) of listening to the Higher Self.

There are people who are more in touch with their Higher Selves than the rest of us. Whether they haven't lost the connection (they kept listening) or they have developed it (started listening again), they have an edge. They are called *channels* or *mediums*. Sometimes they use tools to help them to make more sense of the information they receive, like (Tarot) cards or a pendulum. In the older days, there was a shroud of mystery, darkness, or secrecy surrounding them. This frightened or put off many people.

Nowadays, science, technology and other ways and means (and tools) have been developed or discovered that allow us to tap into the connection with our Higher Self. For example, many doctors, coaches, and therapists use kinesiology to get the input they need to help a patient. The secrecy, odd paranormal connections, darkness, and mystery around intuition are disappearing. The result is more people are beginning to realize that mediums aren't the only channels. We all have our own personal connection with a higher power.

Not everybody receives information from their Higher Self in the same way. Some of us 'see' something, like a vision, images, or internal movie clips. Others 'hear' information as if someone is talking to them. Then there are people who 'know' or 'feel' what is really happening, or what the 'truth' of a situation is. Many times, in business settings or non-spiritual settings, we'll use the term 'gut feeling' or 'intuition' in order to appear more level-headed and normal when talking about things we can't explain.

These different forms of receiving information make being intuitive or in touch with our Higher Self confusing. When we have had an experience with someone who 'hears' the tips from his or her Higher Self, we think that hearing is *the* best or only way of communication. As a consequence, you may be focusing on 'hearing' things and growing frustrated because you keep hearing nothing. Meanwhile, your Higher Self is providing you with rich, abundant visual images you may be ignoring. In other words, you are frantically looking to your right side for the answer, while your Higher Self is standing patiently to your left with all the answers and information you asked for ☺.

Even reading about channeling may tempt you to look for ways to start 'channeling' information and insights more. Or maybe the opposite is true for you: the idea of channeling scares the hell out of you. You want to run away as fast and as far as possible. Either way, it doesn't really matter, because actually, everybody is already receiving pretty clear input from his or her Higher Self on a continuous basis. This is true even if you don't know it.

What do I mean?

First, even when making rather mundane decisions, you are inspired by your Higher Self. For example,

- What do I choose from the menu?
- What shall we name our dog?
- Should I go left or right?
- Are we going to hire this person or not?
- Which clothes will I put on today?

Secondly, you have probably already experienced some feelings today, haven't you? ☺

Whether they are more 'positive', like joy, happiness or excitement, or more 'negative', like sadness, anger or depression, feelings are always nudges from your Higher Self, telling you something about your life.

So how does this work?

It's like the game where you are blindfolded and where other people say 'warm' or 'warmer' when you are closer to your goal and 'cold' or 'colder' when you are farther away from the goal.

In the human game, it is important to keep in mind that the Higher Self wants only the best for Itself, including its Human Form. In other words: your Higher Self wants only the best for you! Your Higher Self nudges you in the 'right' direction, regardless of what that direction may seem to be. When you feel rather 'negative', you are going away from the 'bright future' that your Higher Self, from its helicopter view, sees. When you feel rather 'positive', you are getting closer.

"Closer to what?" you may ask.

Well, in the realm of the Higher Self, it's all about Joy, Peace, and Happiness. That is what your Higher Self wants to share with your Human Form. And that's what it is nudging you towards: "Come closer to Me, come closer to your 'center', because that's where we meet."

Now, what is happening in most human lives? We are living away from our center. We are living in an 'outpost' of our being.

Let me clarify this.

When we incarnate on planet Earth, it is important to make sure the body stays alive. Otherwise, the human game will be over before it has even started ☺. Besides that, the body is such a complex thing that it would cost too much time and energy to have to think of every function (like digestion) or movement (like lifting a finger).

That's why we have a 'battery of small robots' that take care of those things. It is like a car factory: after the robots are programmed to perform certain actions in the assembly line, they perform them automatically, 24 hours a day. In other words: these small robots are there so we don't have to think about every action or reaction. The robots that are responsible for survival are what I call the 'wicked warriors'. They are programmed to look out for danger. When they have spotted danger, they protect us by defending, attacking, or spurring us to run away (whatever seems the best solution at that moment). They live in the outpost.

You could also say the outpost is like an antenna on the extremities of an insect. The little hairs or receivers on the antenna are the wicked warriors.

The wicked warriors are the soldiers in an outpost who ready the guns when they notice something/someone they perceive as a threat. Because there is only a need to attack, defend, or run away when there is a **fear** of something, I call this the fear-based game.

The outpost, with its army of robots, and the wicked warriors of the fear-based game, is what is often referred to as the *ego*. If you're more comfortable using that term, you can do that.

The outpost has a very important function. It helps the body to survive.

What, then, is the problem? The outpost is only a small part of us, but we have strongly identified ourselves with it. It is as if the insect thinks it is the antenna, not the body. Although the antenna is just a small part of who it is, the insect thinks it has become the antenna. Similarly, we have identified with the army of wicked warriors that is permanently on the lookout for danger. In other words, we think we are a small part instead of the bigger entity we really are.

In order to give ourselves a rest and to start living a 'lighter' life (and hence become en-light-ened ☺), it is time to identify ourselves with the bigger part again (which we are connected to in our center). On the one hand, we give the robots another function or role. No longer fear-based, but love-based. In other words, we transform the wicked warriors into merry minstrels.

When we no longer identify with the outpost, we can start identifying again with the creator that we are.

Let me explain this a little more.

The Higher Self is in the realm of 'Being'. At the same time, our Human Form on this three-dimensional planet of space and time is in the realm of 'Doing'. When we are no longer identified with the outpost and more in touch with our Higher Selves, we can start creating again in a conscious way. This is not because we need to survive or defend ourselves, but because creating gives us joy. When we are 'centered', we can easily align with our Higher Self and then take action again. However, this is another kind of action: Inspired Action. This is 'doing' in the physical realm, inspired by 'being' from the non-physical realm.

How does this work?

Our Higher Selves will send us ideas and inspiration in the form of books, people, movies, events, and encounters with elements from nature, places, workshops, etc. Actually, it's continuously doing that, but most of the time we don't see it, feel it, or hear it because our antenna (our army of robots) is/was looking for danger rather than looking for insights, love, or creativity. The ideas, solutions, and love are offered to us from one side, but we are looking to the opposite side.

Giving our robots a new role is a key part in learning to live a 'lighter' life, and to becoming en-light-ened. Even without being aware of it, most of us are so identified with the outpost that changing how we see things is not a simple process. Not only is giving up any identification we already have hard to do, but it is also painful. Our whole life we have relied so much on our outpost for survival that trust and reliance has permeated all parts of our lives. It's not only our physical body, but our mental, energetic, and spiritual bodies we've molded to those beliefs as well. That's why Chapter 2 is dedicated to looking at the various nooks and corners where the wicked warriors are hiding. We don't want to get rid of them. We want to help them to relax. We also want to give them a new role — that of merry minstrels and 'lookers for love'.

Your Higher Self needs feedback from your Human Form in order to keep the Human Form safe and to think about new or alternative strategies.

Although the Higher Self has the helicopter view, it is not 'on the ground' and, as the non-physical part of you, it misses the physical part of the action. In order to help you to have the best possible experience on this three-dimensional planet Your Higher Self needs to receive feedback.

On the one hand, it uses input from your senses — what you smell, taste, hear, see, touch and feel. On the other hand, it seeks out what you want to experience on a spiritual and emotional level. It seeks your desires, goals, and dreams. What do you want to have, do, and be? Your Higher Self can only go out and assemble the right parts — people, places, objects, experiences, etc. — when it has your input.

You've probably already heard about goal setting, vision boards, and how to do these things according to the movie, *The Secret,* or perhaps from some other sources. Goal setting and vision boards are simply a way of making it clear to your Higher Self what you desire to experience or have in your life. However, I have discovered that in most references or books about goal setting or attracting what you want, a few important parts have been omitted or overlooked. As a consequence, many people (including me!) have tried to use goal setting or the Law of Attraction, but we didn't get the results we were looking for. That's why I have dedicated Chapter 5 of this book to explaining how this actually works, what the subtle details are, and how to apply them so you can create a marvelous life for yourself! In Chapter 6 I will even take the concept of the Law of Attraction to a whole new level.

Your Higher Self can communicate with the other Higher Selves to discuss strategies from a helicopter view. The Human Forms only attack/defend the Human Forms from the 'other' team and can heal the Human Forms of their 'own' team.

Many times I imagine a large 'Heavenly Game Room' where our Higher Selves are behind their computers with headphones on their ears or around their necks, legs on the table, drinks and snacks in front of them, talking to each other, laughing and having a lot of fun.

From this game room, our Higher Selves give input to our Human Forms. As and when they receive feedback, they immediately start to work with what they've been given. Because the Higher Self is non-physical, it is not bound by space and time. In other words, the Heavenly Game Room is always open and at our service, 24/7.

Let's look at an example:

Marc is leading a hectic life, running a successful radiator business. He wants to spend more time with his partner Sophie and with his family and friends, but there is always something in the business that keeps him away. His main worry is that he does not have enough money coming in to take care of his family.

I imagine that the conversation in the Heavenly Game Room goes like this:

- *Higher Self Marc: "Ah, my Human Form, 'little' Marc, wants to spend more time with his partner Sophie, family, and friends. OK, I received that request and I'm happy to look for ways to bring this to him. Hmm, what if I had this customer cancel his order, which will free up some space in his calendar. Besides, that customer was not the best match anyway. Let's ask the Higher Self of the CEO of that company, Fred, to play along."*
- *Higher Self Marc: "Higher Self of Fred, do you want to help Marc to have the experience of having more time to spend with his partner Sophie?"*
- *Higher Self Fred: "Sure."*
- *Higher Self Marc: "Can you have Fred cancel the order? That will free up some time."*
- *Higher Self Fred: "Hmm, Fred was actually counting on those radiators. But it is more important that Marc has his experience. So I will find another solution."*

The next day, Fred cancels the order. Marc is livid. "How dare they cancel the order? They are breaching the contract. I'm going to sue them."

(In other words: Marc feels attacked and his first reaction is to retaliate.)

Back in the Heavenly Game Room.

- *Higher Self Fred: "Hmm, this is not working out as planned."*
- *Higher Self Marc: "No, I should have known. Marc is rather tense these days. ☺"*
- *Higher Self Fred: "Can't we find another solution?"*
- *Higher Self Marc: "OK. You can have Fred say that canceling the order was an administrative mistake and that the order is still standing. That won't get Fred into trouble and he doesn't have to find another solution."*
- *Higher Self Fred: "OK. That will work. But how are you going to help Marc to have more time with Sophie, family, and friends?"*
- *Higher Self Marc: "Let's use another strategy. Let's switch from the 'enemy' side to the 'ally' side. Higher Self of Sophie, are you willing to play?"*
- *Higher Self Sophie: "Yes, sure!"*

- *Higher Self Marc: "Let's have Sophie win a holiday trip to Hawaii. That will help Marc to spend some time with her and not have to think about finances at the same time."*
- *Higher Self Sophie: "That sounds like fun!"*
- *Higher Self Marc: "OK, let's do it then. But let's spread it out over time a bit. So much good news all at once may give Marc a heart attack ☺."*

The next day, Fred calls Marc to tell him that there has been a mistake and that they didn't want to cancel the order. Actually, they wanted to order more. The dark clouds in Marc's head immediately disappear. In the evening he comes home and tells Sophie, "You will never guess what happened today. Fred called me personally to apologize. Apparently they made a mistake. The order is still on and they even placed an additional one! Let's celebrate. Let's go to a restaurant." And they have a great evening together.

A week later, Sophie comes home and tells Marc that she has won a vacation to Hawaii. Because that is a location Marc has always dreamt of, he immediately gets his calendar out and blocks two weeks. His mood changes even more. The phone call of Fred a week ago already lifted his spirits. The anticipation of being able to spend two weeks with his beloved partner on a beautiful location puts him in an even better mood.

Every time I think about my life in the way I described in this example, I immediately have to laugh. It instantly lifts my spirits. The consequence is that it is much easier to relax the wicked warriors and look at the world in a different way!

Your Higher Self knows all the necessary elements are there so It can play the game and enjoy the experience. Your Higher Self doesn't question it; It is sure of it, because that's how the game is designed.

In our human lives, all the necessary elements are available to play the human game: people, places, objects, animals, plants, events, etc. However, since we don't have the general overview, and we can't always hear or don't always trust our intuition, we don't always believe that this is so. When we are in the outpost, especially if we are surrounded by our wicked warriors, we don't believe much else is going on rather than what we are seeing with our own eyes.

To use the computer game analogy here, we are not aware of the map our Higher Self is looking at. We can't even see the mini map. We can only see the small area around us. That's how life feels for most people, although there are plenty of examples to contradict this. For example, even when given the example of electricity — we can't see it and don't know how it works, exactly, but we use it all the time, so we know it is there — it is hard to trust that there are things going on around us that we cannot see.

That's why the first step to a lighter life is to come out of the outpost and back into our center.

There it is easier to believe that there is much more going on than what the eyes perceive. In our center it is easier to believe that we can create a magnificent life full of happiness, love, and joy.

Just as in the game *League of Legends*, in one game your Higher Self is competing against a friend, while in the next game that friend can be a beloved teammate. Both versions of the game can provide equal fun!

In each life as a Human Form there are many 'sub games' to be played (or, to use computer game vocabulary, there are 'quests'). We may refer to these sub games as the professional game, the sports/hobby game, the family game, the neighbor's game, the lovers' game, etc. All those games are connected as well, some more loosely than others. They are intertwined even if we aren't aware of it. In some of these 'sub games', we can be teammates, while in others we are adversaries.

For example, let's say you get a new colleague at work and 'accidentally' you discover you both like to play volleyball during lunch. During those lunchtime games, sometimes you are a member of the same team, but most of the time you are not. You really grow fond of each other. Eventually you start dating and, after some time, you marry and start a family. Meanwhile, you have changed jobs and now you work for your spouse's competition. After a few years, you notice you have grown apart, you separate, and eventually divorce. In co-parenthood, you both take care of the children every other week. Due to a merger of the companies some years later, you have to work together again. That's when you discover some other qualities in each other. You've both grown and changed and matured. After a while, the two of you leave that company to start a new, very successful company.

That's not the average life, I know ☺. But it's a good example of how you can be an 'ally' in one kind of sub game and an 'adversary' in another — and how all these sub games are intertwined and can become interwoven in different areas of our lives. And then we are just talking about one lifetime on this planet ☺.

With some Human Forms (in this case: bodies), your Higher Self has a greater affinity than It does with others. One is not better than the other, but they are more suited for your particular experience. Other Higher Selves have other preferences.

You have the right body for your experience in this lifetime. You may not always be happy about how it looks or feels, but it is the perfect body for you to play your human game in this lifetime. Other people have a different body. They have a body that is more suited to their experience. It is, as some may say, "The hand you've been dealt." Not only do you have a unique body, but you have a unique culture, family, birthplace, and so on.

Everybody is here to have their specific experience with their specific body and with their specific situations. This also means that one person's path in life is different than another's. In other words, what's good or bad for me isn't necessarily good or bad for you. Remember the farmer's horse story above? It also means that a specific approach doesn't necessarily work for everybody the same way.

That's why it's important to remember that we don't know:
- What somebody's path is.
- What their background is.
- How they have lived their lives so far.
- What they value.
- What they are looking or longing for.

There is a tendency to judge behavior, beliefs, or points of view that are different from ours. But to be honest, we don't know what caused the behavior or the way someone thinks about something. Not until we start communicating with the intention to understand, rather than the intention to voice our own opinion or to be right, can we begin to get a glimpse of who *they* truly are.

This sounds simple and logical, but because most of us have identified with the wicked warriors of the outpost (which are focused on survival), that is not the way we are used to thinking or interacting with others.

In Chapter 2 I will share tips about how to have different kinds of conversations — conversations in which you can totally be yourself, voice what you are looking for, and improve your relationships at the same time!

The Human Forms don't experience pain when they are hit or die. At least, that is the experience of the Higher Self.

The champions in our computer game analogy don't experience pain when they are hit or when they die. As the player in that game, we don't feel any pain, so we assume there is no pain. The reason why I added this topic is that many people do feel a connection with their Higher Self or with angels, masters, or Source/God, but they feel or believe that they are not heard, or that they are misunderstood when they are heard. They blame the non-physical realm for not relating to their physical or emotional pain, and for not understanding their pain.

For some of you, this may be farfetched, but it may actually be true. Non-physical beings don't have a body, so they don't know what physical pain is. I already have experienced a glimpse of what this is like. From many, many sessions in constellation work (see Chapter 3), I have experienced that a Higher Self doesn't know or doesn't realize that, as Human Forms, we experience emotional and physical pain.

For a Higher Self everything is an experience worth having. Everything is a neutral experience, without 'good' or 'bad', without 'right' or 'wrong', and without emotional pain or physical suffering.

I have to be honest: I was hesitant to add this part to the book, because it sounds rather 'fluffy'. But, while studying both *The Way of Mastery* and some principles from quantum physics, I found the insights that sort of explained what I had experienced during constellations. What I discovered is this: everything **is** neutral. We look at things (objects, people, animals) and then decide to identify with some of them and to value them. When the thing we value as true or important is threatened, we suffer. However, it is not because of what happens to the thing that we suffer, but because of our identification with it and our attachment to the validation of it.

For example, a scratch on a car is a neutral event. But when you look at it as *your* car, you have become identified with it and thus it has emotional value to you as well. And what if you have had to work hard and save a lot of money and sacrifice to get that car? What if you gave up some holiday trips that you really wanted, or did without something else you valued to buy that car? What if you bought the car so you could make your neighbors jealous? Maybe they made you jealous when they bought a new television. Depending on the time, resources and money you've invested in this car of yours, then it may no longer be a scratch on a car, but an assault on you personally! So now anything that happens to it takes on the mission and goal of righting a wrong and engaging in a personal vendetta.

Although there is lots of fighting going on, in the end it is just a way to have an experience you can't have as a Higher Self. It is just a game.

We play a computer game for fun. We are able to test how smart we are (brain, strategy, adventure, puzzle-like games) or how skillful we are (action, shooters, sports-like games) or we play a combination of those. When we win, or play well, our winning or success can provide us with a sense of achievement. When we reach the goals of the game, or perform as we expect to, we continue to accumulate feelings about the game: pride, camaraderie, safety, accomplishment, success, and a feeling of family or tribe with our friends. More and more we understand what is happening to us is because we're playing a game together with other people who get this concept too — both with close friends and with strangers from another place in the world. But not every computer game is about collaboration, peace, joy, and feeling good.

Many computer games are about fighting.

The good thing about computer game that focus on fighting is that most of the time they turn our attention away from real fights or wars. Although you would think that there are many more wars in the world than ever before, especially when you watch the news, the world has actually become a safer place (see for example the short TED talk by Steven Pinker about the myth of violence: **https://www.ted.com/talks/steven_pinker_on_the_myth_of_violence**).

It just seems that there are more wars and an increase in violence because we can read about every small and large event somewhere in the world on mass media and the Internet. Before the Internet, only part of this sum of information reached us, so we had the impression that there was less violence than there actually was.

On the other hand, fights or wars have their origins or causes somewhere. If there wasn't the notion of fighting or war in our consciousness, there wouldn't be any games about it.

So let's dive a little bit deeper into this to see where this war mentality comes from.

Fears

We all have fears. I call them 'monsters'. Some are bigger, some are smaller. Some of them we are aware of, while others remain hidden from us.

Because fears of many different kinds are showing up in our game (our life), we have the opportunity to play with them and transform them. I call that process *transforming monsters into teddy bears* ☺.

Before we can do that, let's look at how fears are created.

When we turn to quantum physics, we learn that there is one large field of energy in which everything in the universe exists. All thoughts float around in this energy. They are neutral thoughts, available to everyone. A part of us picks out certain thoughts. That part of us is not interested in the majority of thoughts — only in a few. The others? It just lets them float by to be seized by someone else. When we have chosen a specific thought, we claim it. We tell ourselves, consciously or not, "This is mine. This is MY thought." In other words, we have identified with it. We now possess it. Next, we put a certain value on that thought (Remember, until the moment we seized it, the thought was neutral). One thought we deem 'true' and another 'false'.

As a consequence, our behavior begins to align with what we have declared true or 'right' and desirable. Our behavior also becomes opposed to the thoughts we've determined to be 'wrong' and despicable.

For example,

"You always need to speak the truth." If you value this as true:
- When somebody is lying, you may become very angry.
- You will probably tell it like it is, regardless of whether this is appropriate in all circumstances. This means you speak the truth even if it is not appropriate to other people, who may feel offended by your speaking your truth. On the other hand, you will probably also get applauded for saying things other people don't dare to say.

"You must always be on time." If you value this as true:
- You will probably always be even a bit too early so you won't be too late.
- You may feel disrespected by people who show up late for your birthday party.

"Money is the root of all evil." If you value this as true:
- You probably won't have much money in your bank account.
- You will be very suspicious of rich people, a potential raise at work, or other opportunities to receive more money.

"Men don't cry." If you value this as true:
- You will hold your tears at all cost. Over time you may even get so good at this that your way of coping is to dissociate from all feelings, both happy ones and the ones that may make you cry.
- You will probably react harshly or be judgmental when you see a boy or man cry. You may even make fun of them to reinforce to yourself that men don't cry.

The higher we value the thought that we have identified with, the more intense our experience is when it shows up in our lives. On top of our values is how the element of time affects and reinforces them. When you think a certain thought long enough, it becomes a belief and is often difficult to confront or dislodge.

So we have intensity plus duration. No wonder people are so passionate or stubborn about certain beliefs ☺.

Now, let's go back to our fears.

I have already explained that we have 'antenna' that hone in on negative thoughts and events, and on potential attackers or perceived threats. These antenna are the wicked warriors of the fear-based game doing what they need to do in their outpost. They are/were used for survival. They are looking for ways to defend themselves against attackers. Their focus is on more than just avoiding the negative feelings. They assume they will be attacked anyway, telling themselves, "It's only a matter of time." Even when something is good now, it surely will be bad in the future, won't it? So they are always on the lookout for negative experiences, even in the good times!

The fear-based game thinking process goes like this:

- All thoughts are neutral and are floating around for everybody.
- I pick one of the thoughts and keep it for myself.
- Now everyone else is mad at me because I picked that thought without asking anyone (I 'stole' the thought).
- Since the others are mad, they are going to come after me to punish me.
- I have to be continually on the lookout so I can defend myself against them.
- Somebody starts talking to me or asks a question.
    - It looks like they are mad. They seem to be attacking me. Now I have to defend myself.
    - It looks like they are not mad, or they are even behaving very kind towards me.
        - They don't know yet that I stole the thought. I must stay vigilant since they may find out any minute I am the thought thief. Then they will attack me.
        - They do know that I stole it, but they are not telling me. They are very cunning. I must stay vigilant, because any minute they can put a knife in my back.

In other words, the wicked warriors are stressed all the time. They constantly fear that they will be attacked.

When we take a deeper look at our fears, we see that fear is always about losing something: losing feeling good, losing being safe, losing being accepted, losing an object, losing our life, losing our health, losing the respect of others, losing our money. Or in other words: we fear that something that we have and value can and will most likely be taken away from us.

Can or do we really possess anything except objects? I don't think so. You can't really possess another human being, a situation, or a feeling. You cannot *be* possessed by them (although it sometimes feels that way ☺). You can be in relationship to them and have emotions about them, but you can't really possess them.

Objects are something else. We can possess objects and fear losing them. But in reality we don't fear losing the objects. We fear losing the experiences and feelings we associate with the objects. We fear that we can't experience them anymore in other ways, or that we have to suffer or sacrifice ourselves again in some way in order to recover or gain the object.

For example, we fear that our car might be stolen. What we actually fear is that we will lose our status symbol (so we lose appreciation). We fear we may lose a means of personal transportation that we can use at any time, so we truly fear losing our independence or freedom. We fear losing a way to make money if we use our car for our work, so we fear our personal as well as our financial survival might be jeopardized if our car is stolen.

Remember that the experience of fear comes from the value we put on the object, person, or situation, as well as our identification with it. Our fears come from our attachment to them; or put differently, we fear that we won't be attached to them any longer. However, what matters is the experience, not the object. And in fact, there are many ways to have that same kind of experience. However, we don't see those possibilities because we are so busy being attached to the things and experiences (objects, people, places) we already know and are familiar with ☺.

For example, there are ways to experience appreciation, independence, and freedom other than with our own car. But because we are familiar and sometimes even stuck with thinking this way, especially when we are stressed, we are focused only on the car and we don't see other options.

How do fears show up?

An interesting part of the game is that fear sometimes doesn't look like fear, because it comes in many other forms and shapes:

- Guilt
- Anxiety
- Despair
- Doubt
- Panic
- Worry
- Uneasiness
- Being overwhelmed
- Being smothered
- Being trapped
- Shame
- And many others

An interesting question to ask ourselves is, "Why are there fears in our life? Why are fears such a significant part of our human game?"

A simple answer is: we need fear to be able to play the game ☺. Without our fears, life wouldn't be so much fun (that's at least the perspective of the Higher Self ☺).

Fears are used to keep us away from our talents and our personal power. Inside the darkness of our shadow side is where these treasures are most often hidden. It is only by 'taking on the quest' that we are able to find those treasures. Fears appear like monsters. They want to overwhelm and destroy us. They keep us away from even attempting to look into the darkness, let alone take time to think there may be a treasure there. Fears (or monsters) discourage us from even attempting to look at the dark cave, let alone enter it.

In order to keep us away from our treasures, our fears need to have different forms and shapes. It would be too easy to find the treasures if there is only one kind of monster. Why? If you had discovered how to disarm, overcome or conquer that one monster and find that one treasure, all the other treasures would be too easily available.

So, what happens? If you had the courage to look at one monster and to defeat it, the next time a different monster appears, you might say: "That first monster I could deal with, but this one seems too big or too frightening to me. I'll just turn around and leave it alone." Because you turned away from the monster you are in less distress, but at the same time you know there is still a monster and you need to be vigilant. That's the role of the wicked warriors: to look out for any monster and any potential danger.

To reiterate: fears (or monsters) are an important part of our game on planet Earth because they show the way to the hidden treasures, namely your talents and personal power.

When you are able to face the monsters, you'll probably first feel overwhelmed, but if you are brave enough, you will discover that they are actually not monsters, but 'wrongly washed teddy bears'. And instead of being scary to you, they become neutral. They may even become your biggest strengths or support mechanisms since they are showing you your treasures in this life.

The question many people have is, "Why do I have to play this game? Why can't I leave the fear-based game right away and not ever have to face the fears and monsters?"

You may not understand it yet, but as the larger being that you are (of which the Human Form and Higher Self are just two aspects), you have deliberately chosen to be here. Part of the game is to not remember this, because then you would know all the answers and it would be no fun to play the game.

Or let's use the computer game metaphor again. Let's assume you just bought a computer game for 30 dollars and you are really looking forward to playing it. You are already excited and anticipating how much fun you are going to have playing it. The first thing you do when you come home is install the game on your computer. After the opening screen you see the character you are going to play with at the left side of the screen.

Now, imagine it is obvious that you have to go to the right side of the screen to continue the game. So you move your character to the right. When you arrive at the right side, you get the message, "Congratulations! You have won the game!" If this happened, you'd be disappointed, if not mad. "What? No obstacles, no quests, no monsters to be slain, no teamwork, no rewards to be gained? No struggles, no chance to prove myself in battle, or to show off my hard won gaming skills?" You feel you have paid 30 dollars for nothing. All the excitement and anticipation about the game's challenges was for naught. You feel cheated. You may even go back to the store, complain, and ask for a refund. In other words, you are not happy with the game at all!

And that's exactly what happens with the human game as well. You, as your Higher Self, would be very disappointed if this human game were as easy to play as moving a character from left to right. We think it would be more fun to have all the answers, but it's not.

Although the human game may seem hard to you at this moment, the good news is that there is support all around you for playing the game. You don't have to do it all by yourself. There is support to become en-light-ened: living a life that is lighter, easier, and more effortless. You will discover that in the next chapter!

The strategies of the wicked warriors

When we go back to the different forms of fear (guilt, despair, anxiety, etc.), it becomes clear that life can be a stressful game. On top of that, it seems that there are so many things to lose every time we turn around. So the wicked warriors must be extra vigilant: "There are so many subtle ways we can be attacked in addition to the obvious, we really need to be on the lookout, 7 days a week, 24 hours a day, 60 minutes an hour, 60 seconds a minute! But no worries, we're prepared!"

To continue using fighting terms and analogies, let's say the wicked warriors have a whole 'arsenal' of tools at their disposal to deal with fear. Those tools are all based on the same foundation: first look for danger, then defend or attack. Some of the tools or strategies are even more subtle than the others.

Let's take a look at what the most popular strategies of the wicked warriors of the fear-based game are:

Strategy 1: Judging

Judging is the result of identifying with certain thoughts and valuing them.

Because it is important to understand what is going on, let's review what I call the 'experience model'.

1. There is a one large field of energy. Everything exists in it.
2. All thoughts float around in this field, and all are neutral and available to everyone.
3. When one of the wicked warriors picks out a thought and identifies with it: "This is MY thought," it becomes activated in our game.
4. Some of the thoughts are valued as 'true' and others as 'false'. As a consequence behavior that is in line with what is true is 'right' and desirable, while unaligned behavior is 'wrong' and despicable.
5. The longer we give attention to a thought, the more it becomes a belief. The more important we deem a belief and the more we identify with it, the more intense our experiences around that thought and the resulting belief will be.
6. Our experience is: the more the thoughts and beliefs that we have valued as 'true' are confirmed, the more relaxed we are (the wicked warriors are at rest). The more that thought or belief is denied or the more the thought that we have valued as 'false' is triggered, the more stressed we are (the wicked warriors are active, they are looking for ways to attack/defend).
7. We react, verbally or physically (or we don't react and keep it to ourselves).

Step 4 is where judgment originates. The moment we label something as 'right' or 'wrong' we have judged something.

The height and severity of our judgment is created in step 5 and 6. These are also the steps that will determine what our physical and verbal actions will be. When our judgment is rather small, we may have an opinion, but we'll keep it to ourselves because to voice it may result in a larger and different threat. When our judgment is a bit bigger, we may complain to others. When we feel emotionally threatened, we may blame someone or even start yelling. When we feel physically threatened, we may run away or stay and start to fight.

When we talk about 'defending against the wrong and despicable stuff', the image of the wicked warriors quite 'naturally' comes up. But, what about 'looking for the right and desirable'? Also when we're looking for the 'right' stuff, the robots are acting like soldiers: everything that is not in line with what the robots perceive as 'right', needs to be attacked as well. Only by destroying the opposite or opposing viewpoint will there be a chance that the 'right' stuff will survive. Only by making the opposite small and powerless can there be a chance that what is right will survive.

In other words; judging and judgment is a never-ending battle.

Strategy 2: Projection

Before we look at projection, first let's have another look at judging.

The moment we start to label some things as 'true' or 'false', what happens is that we automatically start to judge. What is 'true' becomes 'right' and what is 'false' (or the opposite of what is deemed 'right') becomes 'wrong'. The stronger our feelings about that thought, the stronger we're likely to express our judgment with shouting, strong adjectives, superlatives, exaggerations, and accusations (like always or never), etc.

When judgment is about someone's character or personality traits, our reaction looks like this:
- "She is amazingly well mannered. She always wishes me a good morning."
- "He is incredibly dependent on others. He can never do something on his own."
- "She has such good taste. She always wears nice clothes."
- "She is awfully critical. She has always a comment or opinion to voice about everything. Nothing is ever good enough for her."
- "He is so deeply respectful. He always opens the door for me and treats me like a real lady."
- "He is utterly lazy. He never finishes his work on time."

When we talk about judgment, we usually are focused on what we perceive or believe to be the 'negative' about something or someone. Judgment is about things we deem bad, despicable or wrong. It is our judgment about something we value as 'false' or what is opposite to what we value as 'true'.

So why do the wicked warriors value some thoughts as 'wanted behavior or opinions', but also judge some thoughts as 'unwanted behavior or opinions'?

They judge thoughts good or bad, wanted or undesirable, because they relate those thoughts to how to deal with a situation. When the wicked warriors notice something that is in line with what they perceive to be 'true', they deem the situation safe, at least for now. When they notice something that seems 'false' or opposite to what is 'true', an alert about a possible attack goes off. The wicked warriors know that they should start to defend themselves or attack the perpetrator.

One way to defend themselves is to **project** their thoughts, values and fears onto the situation or person.

How does projection work?

Let's say you meet someone and suddenly a thought comes up about this person. The thought you have is that this person believes something that is opposite to what you deem 'true'. The wicked warriors are alerted: "This is someone who wants to attack us!" To avoid being attacked yourself, you use the 'attack is the best defense' strategy and you attack them. This happens when we see people who are different from us. Maybe they're older, younger, black, Asian, male or female, rich or poor, homeless or living in a fabulous mansion with several servants. Whatever it is, there's something about them that triggers our thoughts about them or their character or situation.

For example, you are having dinner with your parents. Before dinner you see your dad lying on the couch. He's relaxing after a hard day of work. Suddenly a thought comes up: "People who work hard become successful" (desired behavior). "It's bad to be lazy!" (despicable behavior). You tell yourself, "My lunch break was a little longer today, but at least it was related to work. I feel so bad about myself now, this really needs to go away, I need to get rid of this feeling. Now look how lazy my dad is, he is just lying on the couch, watching some stupid television show. That is unheard of; no wonder he couldn't give me the toys I wanted as a kid." And suddenly you shout: "Dad, you are always so lazy! When will you start making something of your life?"

Projection is always about something inside ourselves that we don't like. However, instead of looking at it, we separate ourselves from it by dissociating from it. Then we throw it (or project it) onto someone else. Because it is now separated from us and associated with someone else, it is not our problem anymore (at least, that is the strategy of projection). Moreover, the wicked warriors can now defend themselves against it so it won't come back to haunt or disturb us. When we dissociate the experience, there is no relationship with it anymore, at least not for us. As a consequence our projection can be attacked; it can be seen as worthless; it can be disposed of and best of all, it can be seen as someone else's issue or problem, allowing us to escape the pain of owning it in ourselves.

Strategy 3: Victimhood

When we feel attacked, most of us fall into a **victim** role. We tell ourselves, "Poor me, they are attacking me, it is not fair."

Complaining about it is one of the most common ways to deal with this feeling of unfairness. It is about justifying our victimhood. The reason behind being a victim is the strategy of "I know, you are mad (and you have all the more reason for it, because I have stolen the thought), but look at how small I am, it is not my fault. I shouldn't be punished."

Most of us step into the victim role easily enough, but we do so even more quickly if it looks like the attacker or the threat seems too big or too overwhelming to do anything without being physically or mentally hurt. In other cases, we take a different approach. When we perceive the attacker as smaller or when we realize he is not aware yet that we perceive him as an attacker we are more likely to attack. We attack because in those cases attack seems to be the best defense, especially when we can add an element of surprise. Then something really interesting happens: to get out of the victim role (defending ourselves), we step into the **persecutor** role (attacking others).

The idea behind this strategy is: by attacking the other person, we take away their (potential) power to attack us. We 'weaken' them. Although it seems that our launching an initial attack will keep us 'safe', that approach creates a very unstable situation. The person we've just attacked (verbally or physically) may suddenly find some extra ammunition, power or resources somewhere and come back much stronger and attack us. In other words, we need to be vigilant all the time.

A 'subtle' variation of becoming the persecutor is becoming the **rescuer**. Although most of the time the rescuer-victim relationship is seen as the positive version of the persecutor-victim relationship, it is more or less the same.

The idea behind this victim-rescuer strategy is: we perceive someone as weak, so we become their rescuer; we make or keep the other one small so they don't have enough power to attack us.

When you read about these victim-persecutor/rescuer strategies, you may think: "That's not how I behave. Or at least not intentionally." Exactly! Most of us end up in the victim-persecutor or victim-rescuer relationship in a very subtle, almost unconscious way.

For example:

When you get a fine for speeding, how do you react? Don't you feel like a victim most of the time? And what thoughts are going through your mind? Are you thinking something like: "I will go over there and explain what happened. Then they will shut up and throw the fine away!" At the same time you know that that action won't work. You understand that it's about bureaucracy, which feels unfair to you at the time, so you end up feeling overwhelmed and powerless. You may think to yourself, "They should do something with my tax money other than fine innocent people like myself!" If you're truly angry you may tell yourself, "The next time I see a police van, I will follow them, and if they park a few centimeter on the curb, or do anything remotely illegal or offensive, I will take a picture and put it on Facebook. That will teach them!" (Sounds like attacking, no? ☺)

Another example:

Paul is on holiday and waiting to cross the street. He suddenly sees a woman in a wheelchair. He immediately thinks that she will have problems crossing the street. So he goes over to her and says: "Let me help you cross the street." The lady reacts in a hostile way: "Leave me alone, I can do it by myself."

What happened? Because Paul made the assumption that this person was in need of something and that he is the only one who can provide that help, he makes himself a rescuer and the woman a victim. Because she doesn't want to be put in the victim position, she defends herself.

How could Paul have dealt with it differently? Instead of making the assumption that the lady needed help, he could have asked: "Do you need any assistance in crossing the street?" In this way, there is no victim-rescuer game at play and both parties are free to choose whether to seek assistance and whether to offer help.

The victim-persecutor/rescuer game can indeed be subtle, can't it? No wonder the wicked warriors love playing it ☺.

Combined strategies

The feeling of being attacked goes even further than simply meeting a person. You can also be triggered by something you read on the Internet or hear on the radio. It is a statement that you deem 'wrong' or that is opposite of what you deem desirable. This gives you a bad feeling. But you don't want to feel bad. You want to get rid of this emotion. And how do people do this in general? By complaining to others in person, writing a blog post about it or posting a comment on Facebook where they blame someone for the feeling this event, news, photo or person has triggered in them.

For example:
- You hear on the radio that taxes will be increased. You feel personally attacked because 'they' are going to take away your money. You complain about it to your colleague at work: "Those politicians should work some more themselves and be paid a lot less!" Now your colleague, whose dear cousin is a local politician answers, "Maybe it is time you start working a little bit harder yourself."
- You read on Facebook an article about fights in Israel and Palestine. You are emotionally attached to one of the two sides and react by defending it: "They are allowed to use violence because the other one started!" In a matter of minutes you get a bunch of 'hate responses' and comments such as, "If you defend their case you are a criminal yourself and you should be hanged."

What happens in general when you blame or complain?

People will go along with you and add to the blaming and complaining. Or you will get a negative reaction and be attacked by people on the opposite side of the event or news. Both situations only strengthen your belief that your feelings or position certainly must have been true, and that your blaming and complaining was justified. All the time the other people were just minding their own business — thinking about other things. As far as 'retaliation', none of them had any intention whatsoever of attacking you until you started it. In other words, your words and actions have become a self-fulfilling prophecy.

Let's look at the case of the 'retaliation' for your stating your opinion or stance, or expressing your thoughts about something. The attack/defense cycle has now started. Because they 'attacked' you, you now feel even more like a victim. So, you feel a need to defend yourself even more by reacting stronger and stronger to them. Then they retaliate, the situation escalates and the vicious cycle continues.

When you read about the different strategies of the wicked warriors and realize how tiresome it must be to be a non-stop, vigilant warrior, you see it's no wonder so many people feel tired all the time, burn out, and have a 'short fuse'.

On the other hand, when you look at the whole 'fear-based game' itself, you have to admit that the way it is constructed is fabulous. Not only the mechanics of how it works, but the lengths we go to in order to cover it up make this a fantastic, inventive and most amazing game! ☺

The good news about the human game is that the solution to transform the fear-based strategies into love-based strategies is already built into the game. We have all the clues to get out of the fear-based game on our life path. What are those clues? Let's call them teddy bears disguised as monsters. In a computer game those clues are the reward (gold, items, clues) you get for slaying a creature or fulfilling a quest. Also, in every negative experience in life there is a nugget of gold, a positive experience, that leads in the right direction as long as you are willing to look at it.

After having looked at the strategies of the wicked warriors, it's time to take a deeper look at how the human game works.

The human game in a larger perspective: the 3 Phases of Life

What is this game we are playing on Earth about?

It is about getting to know ourselves better.

I already mentioned that our Human Form and our Higher Self are part of a larger Non-physical Infinite Being, which Itself is connected to God/Source and consequently to everything else that exists. This Infinite Being wants to play a game. It wants to explore how it feels to NOT be connected as well as how to create things from a physical point of view.

So, similar to the computer game characters we, as human beings, have created in order to have a variety of experiences (like being a hobbit, a racecar driver or a superhero), our Infinite Beings created Human Forms to have certain experiences.

In order to play the game our Infinite Beings needed to limit themselves. They did this by creating a condensed form (body) that lives in a dimension of space and time. In order to stay in communication, a liaison was created: the Higher Self. At the same time the limits were created, characteristics were added that are not available when in a non-physical form. We don't have senses as an infinite Being and we don't know what it is like to feel separate. So the human game gives us the opportunity to explore what feelings are like. We can also look at other bodies, objects, animals, flowers like separate things.

Now, let's look at how the human game is constructed.

It exists of three phases:

The **first phase** of the game is to explore what it is like to live as **a separate being**. In order to fully enjoy this part of the game of being an individual, we also put a veil over the connection with our Higher Selves so we are unaware of the game itself. In order to play this phase of the game, we need the wicked warriors in the outpost.

The **second phase** is to start **remembering the human game**. In this phase we sometimes feel the connection with our Higher Selves, but most of the time we don't. This is the phase in which we look to remember the Oneness and to 'heal' the thoughts of separation. We start seeing clues about this connection by coming across things like books, workshops or people who say things to us that resonate with us, even if they don't quite make sense at the time. We start to feel the connection again. In this phase it is about relaxing the wicked warriors, turning them into merry minstrels and then working together with our Higher Self to feel the Oneness again.

The **third phase** of the human game is to **fully work together with our Higher Selves**. As conscious physical parts of the Non-physical Infinite Being we remember our powers as incredible creators. We are here to enjoy the Joyful Game of Life, a game in which we focus on extending life and love. In this phase we are consciously aware of our connection with Source, while still being in a human body.

To use the computer game analogy again: in phase 3 we create, together with our Higher Selves, extra levels, quests or maps. Or, we can even create a whole new game together!

What is the purpose of the human game? To play the game ☺. To have the experiences, to start remembering, to feel the connection again, to feel the Oneness again. To have joy. To create new experiences, objects, events and to enjoy them. Enjoying the process of creating the experiences and the fruits of the process is what it's all about.

Actually the human game is similar to any other game—achieve a goal while enjoying the process of playing. Every game has a goal, but the actual purpose of a game is about enjoying playing it. We are to enjoy the experiences it provides, the opportunities to interact and connect with others, and to learn so we can engage even more in future games.

For example,
- The board game of *Monopoly*: the goal is to have the most money at the end. What is the purpose? To enjoy the experience of buying, selling and strategizing.
- The sports game of basketball: the goal is to have more points at the end of the game than the other team. What is the purpose? To enjoy the experience, to test one's skills against other skilled players, and to get better so we can enjoy the next game even more.
- In the computer game of *League of Legends* the goal is to capture the other team's fortress. What is the purpose? To enjoy the experience, the camaraderie and connections with others as we do so.

The biggest problem in the human game for most people is that they don't remember that they chose to play the game. They forgot they wanted this experience as an infinite Being and that at the time they chose it, they really looked forward to having this experience. Once here however, they identified so much with the limited body in the limited dimension of planet Earth in space and time that they forgot the goal of the game. They forgot that they put clues in place to show them the way in case they had forgotten. Actually they are playing the first phase of the game so well, that they rarely get to the second phase.

I think it must be very interesting from the perspective of our Higher Selves. I can imagine some Higher Selves in the Heavenly Game Room have a conversation like this:

- *"Isn't it time for your Human Form to go the second phase of the game?"*
- *"Yes, it is, but my character, my Human Form, keeps 'bumping into the trees' when I try to steer him away from them. I'm having him feel 'negative' emotions about the situation and have him look the other way, but it's not working like I thought."*
- *"Will I help and have my Human Form go over to him and tell him it is time to play the second phase of the game? Actually, that was what we agreed upon beforehand: that my Human Form would pass on a clue in case your Human Form had forgotten."*
- *"OK."*
- *"Wow, my Human Form told him what the second phase of the game was and he didn't believe it at all. He must still be enjoying the first phase of the game."*
- *"Yes, he loves the deep immersion in the fear-based game of Phase 1. ☺"*
- *"Did he leave other clues for himself to be reminded?"*
- *"Yes, he did. There is actually a whole range of books, workshops, people, and events that are set up for him to discover."*
- *"OK. Let's see what may work then. Let's ask the Higher Self of his mother to have her Human Form to give him one of the books he left as a clue for himself."*
- *"OK."*
- *"Wow, that didn't work either. He got the book, put it in his library and never looked at it. But hey, maybe the seed is planted and maybe he will read it later on."*
- *"Do you have any more ideas? I try to guide him via his emotions, but he keeps going for the experiences that make him feel bad. He probably doesn't know yet that it works this way."*
- *"What about his company organizing the workshop he has left as a clue for himself?"*
- *"That's a good idea! Let's also ask the Higher Self of Peter (someone he chose to be a clue as well) to have his Human Form be a participant and to give him this clue. So he will have two clues in one experience."*
- *"Pfff, your Human Form is a hard nut to crack ☺. He also didn't get those two clues. But wait, something is changing. I saw him looking at the book he got from his mother. It looks like he is starting to remember something. Let's give him some more time. And let's see which other clues we can give him."*
- *"Yes! I have all the time in the world (since I'm infinite I don't even know what time is ☺). And I'm having fun no matter which phase of the game we are in!"*

I think they must be laughing very hard at the stubborn determination so many of us have when we insist on continuing to play the fear-based game of phase 1!

Let's sum up how the human game goes:

Step 1. You start with a character (this is your body and the talents you are aware of).

Step 2. You go 'on the road' and meet obstacles (fears) and aid (support from other people or more awareness of perhaps hidden talents). In the first phase you are not consciously aware of them yet.

Step 3. After a while you arrive in phase 2 of the game. You are still 'on the road', but now you are remembering the game, finding extra talents or discovering clues that remind you of the game you agreed to play. If you are brave enough, you look at the fears and perceive them as monsters.

Then there are two options:
- If you are brave enough to REALLY look at the monsters, you will discover they are 'wrongly washed teddy bears'. You do this by relaxing the wicked warriors and transforming the monsters into teddy bears.
- If you are not brave enough to REALLY look at the monsters, you will run away towards the 'road' again, only to meet the same fears and monsters on another crossing or to meet other fears or monsters (or in another disguise).

Step 4. Every time you face the fears and monsters and transform them into teddy bears, you become stronger and have more courage to face the next fears and monsters. And at the same time you become lighter and lighter. Ultimately, you become more en-light-ened.

Step 5. After a while you enter phase 3. You consciously connect with your Higher Self and together you consciously and joyfully create new objects, situations and experiences.

"What if I don't go to phase 2 or 3 in my life?" you may ask.

No worries; you are already in phase 2, or you wouldn't be reading this book ☺.

Actually it doesn't matter what phase we are in when we leave the body and pass over. Our Infinite Being can play this game again with another body, in other circumstances, with other fears, monsters, teddy bears, allies, enemies. Although it looks as if, when the body dies, the game is over once and for all, we do come back lifetime after lifetime to play the human game. We do this until our Infinite Being has explored and experienced everything it wanted to explore and experience on planet Earth. Then we are 'really' enlightened and don't come back in a physical form anymore.

The rest of this book is about assisting you in playing the human game. I assume you are already very good at playing the Phase 1 game, so let's skip that part ☺ and focus on Phase 2 and 3. In other words: in the remainder of the book you will find lots of tips to relax the wicked warriors and turn them into merry minstrels. You'll also learn to transform monsters into teddy bears, to connect with your Higher Self and to play the Joyful Game of Life!

Chapter 2: Becoming Lighter

You may feel a great deal of despair when reading all the details about the Phase 1 game (with the outpost full of wicked warriors). You may think, "That's not what I want, but it all seems too much or too complicated to change."

Rest assured. You can play another game, if you want to.

Your first step in fleeing fear, and an outpost of wicked warriors, is to decide that you want to play another game. You don't want the fear-based game of life, but the Joyful Game of Life.

Actually the only step you need in changing any game you're playing is making the decision to play a different game. It's quite like changing an outfit you don't like as much as you thought when you put it on. The decision is easy. However, from my own life experience, I know the actual act of changing a game is not always that easy. I, for instance, was 'distracted' by the Phase 1 game (and I still am distracted by it on a very regular basis ☺). So I discovered it was easier to choose for the Joyful Game of Life when the old Phase 1 game was not pulling so hard at me anymore.

So let's see how we can loosen up the wicked warriors, get them out of a cramp, have them relax a bit and help them take their place as the helpful scouts for loving thoughts (by turning them into merry minstrels). Let's go on a small journey to discover where the wicked warriors have been hiding in your whole system: body, mind, beliefs, emotions, values, etc. This may seem like a hard task, but you can actually approach it like a fun game in itself! This chapter of the book will show you how to do this.

Once you have cleaned up your system and you are not longer playing the Phase 1 game or using survival patterns, you can create your Joyful Game of Life. You may also create your Joyful Game of Life while you're in the process of cleaning up your system, depending on your preferences. Remember, we all play our own game, in our own ways, and no two lives are the same! I will provide more detail on that in Chapters 4, 5 and 6.

In other words, in Chapter 2 is about looking at the 'arsenal' of the wicked warriors, dismantling all their weapons, and offering them alternatives, which will lead to a first level of more lightness and happiness!

Invitation 1: Look at planet Earth as the neutral game board

Although it may be hard to believe, everything that happens in your life is because you created it. All the decisions you've made or not made, all the jobs you took, people you've met or become involved with... you are who you are and where you are because, on many levels in many ways, you created it.

We have already seen the bigger picture of the human game. Let's look at some more details of how the game is created.

Before you came to planet Earth, certain conditions were set up. When you were still in a non-physical form, you chose the parents, family, region, culture, etc. that were the best match for your game in this lifetime. You created the best conditions to have different kinds of experiences: things you would like and things you wouldn't like. You also asked others to play the game with you and to assume the role of adversary, ally or resource in your game.

From the moment you were born, all the things you set up before you were born started to play out. However, since you only wanted to play a game that was exciting and challenging and fun, you deliberately forgot that you had made agreements with other people. And you also forgot that you had looked forward to a dimension in which you could perceive duality. It's from that dimension of duality you can create your specific experience: I want this, but I don't want that.

What also happened, is that you were thrown into the outpost and identified yourself with it. The result is that you feel duality as a threat: you judge things, people and events. Instead of just picking what you want from the buffet, you start judging the buffet: that soup is 'bad', those fries are 'good', that sandwich is 'bad', that ice cream is 'good', etc.

From a worldly perspective, that approach to life happened because you learned it from your parents, who learned it from their parents, and so on. They are used to playing the game this way so that is how they taught you to play the game as well. In other words, you observed your parents, siblings, and your larger community and took over some of their survival patterns. You programmed your wicked warriors according to the things you picked up from your environment.

Although this is the (subconscious) reason many of us are mad at our parents and why many psychologists and psychiatrists look at childhood to find the causes of trauma, the fact is this is part of the game **you** chose to play.

When you were preparing your current life on planet Earth, the non-physical beings that helped you with that process explained the process: "When you go to planet Earth to play the human game, you will start your life in the outpost instead of your center. And since you want to play this game fully immersed, you will forget that you prepared it yourself and that you have set up the game like this. In your Human Form you may even suffer physically." Then they asked the most important question: "Do you still want to go in and play the game?" Because you didn't have a clue what duality, the fear-based game or physical pain was when you were still in your non-physical form, you naively answered: "Yes, bring it on. I want to play this game, I look forward to it, I'm excited about it."

Then your helpers asked: "Are you sure about this? You will forget that you have planned it yourself. You will begin your life in a fear-based environment. This will ensure that you will act from this fear-based energy when you realize that there must be some other way to do this. However, you will have forgotten about those other ways and you will start to blame people, especially the ones closest to you. There is a sort of remembering inside you, something that tells you they hold a key that can help you, but you will have forgotten what that key looks like. And since the only way you can ask for help from a fear-based energy is to attack and defend, they will respond with attacking and defending as well. So we ask you again: do you really want to take on a Human Form?"

At this moment you start to doubt a bit, because now you realize that you may be hurting your heavenly friends, the ones that have also taken on a Human Form. So you ask: "Is there a way I can play the human game and do it in a gentle way?" Your helpers responded: "There is a way. You can choose to hide energy sources that will assist you and clues that will help you remember find your way back. Meaning: there's a way you can regain your understanding about why you are on Earth." You answer: "That sounds like a good idea. However I don't want the energy sources to be too obvious, otherwise I may not enjoy the game as much."

The helpers respond: "What you can do is to hide the clues and the keys in plain sight. You can put your energy sources around you, but disguise them so you won't immediately look for them in those hiding places. You can hide them in the dark corners of your being and dress them up like monsters so you aren't attracted to them. However, the result is that you will be afraid of them. Only in your moments of distress, when you don't see any other way out, you will go there. And when you REALLY look at the monsters, they will reveal themselves to you as the loving teddy bears (pointers to your energy sources) they have always been."

You answer: "That sounds like an excellent idea. However, what if those monsters look too scary? What if I don't dare to look at them? Can I have an extra helpline?" The helpers respond: "Yes. You can hide extra clues and hints for yourself. For example, you can hide them in books, in songs, in movies, in what people say or write to you. You can also work with your Higher Self to point you to these clues." You answer: "Great! That should do it! Now I'm ready to go for it! Let's play the game!"

To sum things up:
- You created your game up front before you were born. You have chosen the neutral game board of planet Earth to play your human game.
- You left 'energy sources' for yourself in the form of teddy bears, but disguised them as monsters.
- You left clues and hints in the form of books, songs, things people say or write, etc.
- You have your Higher Self as your scout to point you in the direction of the clues.
- You continue to create your life afterwards by making choices: I want this and I don't want that. (They truly are neutral choices, but due to the Phase 1 game you judge things as 'right' or 'wrong').

In other words: **you** have created your life. **You** have made the decisions. No one else did. As a consequence it's only logical for you to assume total responsibility for your life. No one has done anything to you. They are only responding to your request to play the game with you. They are just showing you the clues you created before you were born. Those clues may be the trigger of an emotional reaction that may lead to a monster in need of transformation into a teddy bear, but they are not the cause. They are your help lines — sometimes disguised as enemies. They are disguised that way only because that's how you wanted to have the clue presented to you.

The invitation here is, don't make yourself a victim any longer and don't make other people the persecutors or rescuers. Take complete responsibility for your life. Take back the power that you have given away to others (usually without them wanting it). It is your life. When you stop blaming others, your life will become lighter and quieter on its own. You will float from the outpost to the center without having to DO anything. Enjoy the ride ☺.

Planet Earth as the game board

So you wanted to play a game and you needed a place to do that. The three-dimensional planet Earth apparently looked like it would serve that purpose. So Earth had the privilege to be chosen by you as the game board for your game.

Just like a game board in any game, the planet Earth is a neutral place. The game of *Monopoly*, for instance, is a cardboard board. The *League of Legends* game takes place in an online environment. For both games, the 'board' is neutral.

On the game board of planet Earth there are only neutral events (which we can then value and identify with). In reality, nobody is attacking you or anyone else. Although the wicked warriors may now scream out loud: "This is not true. Look at the world and all the people in it. They are constantly attacking each other. They are constantly attacking me! I need to defend myself!" If you identify with that small part in you, then that is the only way to look at the world. And yes, if you look at the mass media, this image is only reinforced.

But is this what is really going on?

What I have learned from quantum physics on the science side and *The Way Of Mastery* and *A Course In Miracles* on the spiritual side is that we can also choose to look at the world in a different way to discover its real image.

Remember the 'experience' model from Chapter 1 where I described how we create our experience? There we saw that everything is neutral until we identify with it and value it.

I invite you to look at the world as it is — a neutral playing field. Let's look at it as the neutral game board it truly is. Remember, all events on the board are neutral. It simply provides us with a place to play our game and to create our experiences. If you still have a hard time grasping this concept remember the story of the farmer and his son. Other people judged situations as good or bad, but the farmer was able to see all events as neutral events.

The invitation is: next time something happens that you deem a good or bad thing, take a step back and assume the position of the witness. Ask yourself:

1. **What actually happened**? Can you describe it in neutral, objective words (non-emotional)?
2. **Did it trigger you**? If so, why? Did you feel attacked? And are your wicked warriors triggered? Avoid identifying with them and keep looking at the event or person from the independent view of the witness.
3. **Is the other person triggered**? Is it possible that he or she has another background or history (including emotions) that makes him or her look at events from another point of view? Is it possible that his or her reaction triggered something in you that is not related to the event? A good thing to remember: people and events can often be a trigger, not the cause!
4. **After looking at the emotional parts, can you look at the event again and describe it in even more neutral, objective words?**

Of course this is not always easy to do, especially when one or more parties are emotionally triggered and their wicked warriors are in full harness and battle gear, ready to attack or defend.

Extra tip: when I become aware (which often is not at the beginning of this process) that I've stepped into a pitfall, or that the conversation has gone in the direction of a fear-based battle, I will ask for a time out. While in that time out I ask myself the questions above.

What typically happens is that I first become aware of the anger, grief, rejection or resentment I am feeling in the moment. These emotions are all weapons of the wicked warriors. Then I begin to look at the event in a more neutral way. Thereafter the emotions cool down a bit. Finally, I'm able to choose to open myself up and talk about what really happened without the wicked warriors interrupting and reacting. Most of the time I'm then able to act from a centered perspective. However, being able to stop reacting from the outpost is already enough to turn the situation around.

Let me share with you an example from my own life. A few months ago, Gwendolyn (my partner) and I were having a conversation about where to live. Because there are many parameters involved (house, shop, us, children), this is a sub game that is rather complex. It has given Gwendolyn many days and nights of worry. When I threw in that I needed 'my own space' in the house and that I didn't see how that would work out, something was triggered in her. She felt hurt and went into fear-based survival mode. I was sucked in to that fear as well. After 10 minutes of a more heated and emotional discussion I realized what had happened and asked for a time-out.

Then I asked myself the questions:

1. **What actually happened?** "We had a discussion about where to live."
2. **Did it trigger you?** "Yes, a monster showed up. The monster was the fear that there would not be enough 'me space' in the house. Or rather, that my desire for the 'me space' was not heard."
3. **Is the other person triggered?** "Yes, it looks like she was triggered because I made the situation too difficult. Or, she may have been triggered because she thought that her children were not seen enough. But these are guesses. I saw that she was triggered and I know that I was not the cause. So I don't have to take it personally. I also don't know all of her history and background, so actually I may be interpreting everything in the wrong way."
4. **After looking at the emotional parts, can you look at the event again and describe it in even more neutral, objective words?** "We are having a conversation on how we can live together in the best possible way for everybody involved. There are some old pains or monsters being triggered, but I know she is not the cause of my monsters and I'm not the cause of hers. I'm willing to look at things differently. I choose to leave the wicked warrior outpost."

This helped me return to my center. Due to the fact that the discussion was not fed with more arguments or emotions Gwendolyn calmed down a bit as well. Besides being able to assess the situation from a different point of view from my center, it also allowed me to think about the bigger human game and my intention. So I said to myself: "I'm Love and you are Love. My intention is for everybody involved to be happy." Then I apologized for having been in my outpost, playing the Phase 1 game. Without me pointing out anything, this made her realize that she had been doing the same thing. Suddenly the energy shifted. She was also able to quickly leave her outpost. This shift from her outpost to the center, together with my sharing that she had triggered me, but that she wasn't the cause of how I felt, turned the situation around. The result was a constructive conversation in which we felt each other's understanding for each person's needs and the love that is between us.

Invitation 2: Be grateful for the roles other people play

Other people play roles in your game

When you play a computer game that involves other characters, whether human players or computer controlled characters, each has different roles.

Why are they in the game? To help you play and enjoy the game. They assume one or more of these roles:

1. As an **enemy/adversary**: you can test your skills by competing with them. When you defeat them, you get a reward. Or you can continue on your quest, grow in strength, rise a level, or gain more skills and abilities.
2. As an **ally**: they are by your side, defeating the enemy together with you or helping you fulfill your quest. Sometimes they have skills you don't have. Sometimes those skills are complementary and are needed to achieve a goal. They may also cheer you on and celebrate your joint successes.
3. As a **resource**: they give you clues, helpful tips or items that make your journey easier and lighter.

The people in our lives play similar roles.

Role 1: We perceive them as an 'enemy/adversary'.

The people who are in this role bring you gifts, although they don't seem like gifts at all (and with them not being fully aware of their role either). However, they contain the rewards, the 'helium gas' that makes us lighter. They trigger the monsters in us so they can be transformed into teddy bears.

There are several ways they do this:

* Mirroring how you think or feel about things. Many times we are not aware of how we feel or think about events, situations, people, etc. It's only in interaction with others that our thoughts and feelings are confirmed, challenged, or even brought to light.
* Triggering an old pain or painful experience: since we didn't see the gift in the past, they are here to show the same topic again and again until we do.
* Triggering a belief or value: they question something we value positively or they firmly proclaim something we value negatively.
* Showing what lives inside us by what we have projected onto them, or mirroring our behavior towards others.
* Showing us where we have given away our power or where we haven't grasped it (victim-rescuer/persecutor games).

The gift is always that they show us where there is still a fear-based part in us so it doesn't have to show up in another way (via an illness for example).

However, when we don't know how to play the game, we are afraid of these people. We don't see the gifts. They seem like dreadful hand grenades instead of delightful presents. So we don't accept them, but attack the 'enemy/adversary' instead of being grateful for the gift they have brought us. In many cases those people haven't consciously assumed the role of 'enemy/adversary' when they decided to interact with us. So they feel surprised and betrayed when we perceive them as such. Many times the only way they know how to respond to our attack is to retaliate with an even more vicious counter attack. "Hey, I just came to deliver this gift, I didn't want to attack you, but since you are attacking me, you leave me no other choice than to retaliate." And so the cycle begins.

Role 2: We perceive them as an 'ally'.

These are the people who are by our side, share experiences with us, who help us out, offer a shoulder to cry on and show what love in Human Form can be.

However the pitfall here is that we see them as our rescuers. And then we play another form of the Phase 1 game.

Role 3: We perceive them as a 'resource'.

These are the people who point to interesting books, websites, articles, and tips that help us on our quests. We may know them personally, but sometimes they are public authors, journalists, coaches or therapists. They share their insights via various media, or their own website. They also point us to other useful resources.

On the other hand many times the 'resources' are strangers you 'accidentally' meet at a workshop, presentation, fair, birthday party or event. The event doesn't matter as much as the seemingly chance encounter with someone who points to, or hands you a clue for your path in life.

What does this look like for me?

Sometimes I imagine our Higher Selves sitting together in the Heavenly Game Room assisting their Human Forms. For example my Higher Self is trying to help me and having a conversation that goes something like this:

58

- *Higher Self Jan: "Oh my Human Form, 'little' Jan, wants to learn more of what it is like to live from his center and less from his outpost. Who is willing to participate in creating an experience for him?"*
- *Higher Self-mother Jan: "I want to participate, but my Human Form is now playing another game and is not available for the moment."*
- *Higher Selves father Jan, family, friends: "The same here."*
- *Higher Self-Gwendolyn: "My Human Form is available, but we've already scheduled another experience for next week. It doesn't seem a good idea to have both of them. That may be too confusing."*
- *Higher Self-Jan: "I agree. Anyone else available?"*
- *Higher Self-owner of the office: "Yes, my Human Form is available."*
- *Higher Self-Jan: "OK. Let's create an experience together. Our Human Forms don't have a close relationship, but they get along well. So let's create a shock and see if Jan will be able to stay/go in his center and not react from his outpost."*
- *Higher Self-owner office: "I don't know, because I don't want my Human Form and Jan to have a fight. I don't want any of them to feel hurt."*
- *Higher Self-Jan: "I agree, but it seems the only way to really test it. Do you want to risk it? I think it will be an exciting experience for both Human Forms!"*
- *Higher Self-office owner: "I want Jan to have this experience. Out of love I will do it. Whatever the consequences are."*
- *Higher Self-Jan: "Great! Let's throw in a clue for your Human Form as well!"*
- *Higher Self-office owner: "It's not scheduled for now, but why not? It's not necessary, because I want to do this for Jan, but if my Human Form can get a clue for his own path, that would be great!"*

What happened in the three-dimensional world? At the end of the lease of the office, the owner and his wife came by and started to complain about many tiny damages. They asked for a significant amount of extra money. This was totally unexpected and came as a shock. It also felt like a big assault on me. In the moment I was able to keep calm and reacted in a rather neutral way, but afterwards I was shaking and angry. The first thing that came to mind was: "How dare they? I will teach them a lesson!" Several attack scenarios came to my mind.

Then I suddenly realized that I had fallen into the victim-persecutor trap. They felt so much like victims that they made me the persecutor. And they did it with so much energy that I was sucked in immediately. When I realized what was going on, I started to see them in a different light. I became mild towards them and towards myself. I floated towards my center and was able to reach it. As a consequence I was able to figure out a solution that would be acceptable for both parties. This would never have happened when I was still in my outpost, playing the fear-based game of victim-persecutor.

Two weeks later, something very interesting happened. A mutual acquaintance told me that she met the office owner and that he told her that I had been very inspirational to him. When I asked her what he had said specifically, she answered: "The only thing he said is that he is very inspired by the way you live your life and how you look at things." The interesting part is that I only talked about the solution, not about the outpost, center, or victim-persecutor game. In other words, the only thing that he could have experienced was the shift inside of me!

I can only guess what happened in the Heavenly Game Room, but I assume the conversation might have been something like this:

- *Higher Self-Jan: "Wow, what an excellent experience!"*
- *Higher Self-office owner: "It was a close call, but it worked."*
- *Higher Self-Jan: "Yes, thank you very much!"*
- *Higher Self-office owner: "And my Human Form also discovered one of his clues as well. That's a nice bonus!"*
- *Higher Self-Jan: "Yeah, I love it when a plan comes together! ☺"*

Don't take it personally

Above, I described the roles other people play in our lives. We also play these roles in their lives:
1. Enemy/adversary
2. Ally
3. Resource

I already explained that most other people are so immersed in playing their Phase 1 game that they don't realize they are playing a specific role in someone else's life. As I explained in the part about the enemy/adversary role, they are not aware that they have that effect on you. When you attack them, they retaliate on automatic pilot because they are caught off guard and their wicked warriors, responsible for survival, take over. The same is happening to them: they might perceive you are playing the enemy/adversary role, while you have no idea.

So when they attack, it is because they feel threatened, not because you have intentionally done anything, or deliberately attacked them. That's why this invitation is to not take anything personally. When people react, most of the time it is because you have unconsciously triggered something within them. Not because you are doing something wrong or because you are a bad person.

This coin has two sides. Let's look at the roles of 'ally' and 'resource'. We gladly take credit for playing those roles because our wicked warriors see this as relief, as a temporary sign of approval.

But it is the same as the 'enemy/adversary' role: most of the time we are not the cause of it, we are just the trigger. Although this may be a hard task if you want to relax the wicked warriors: the attachment to these roles needs to be released as well.

In short, don't take things personally, whether it seems to you to be 'good' or 'bad' at the time.

Now, does this mean that we can't help people anymore? Of course not. But I invite you to look at which point of view you do this: from the Phase 1 position (outpost) or from the love-based Phase 2 or 3 position (center). If you are looking at it from the centered position, you will notice that you actually don't care whether or not it is seen what you have done. You don't need approval anymore for what you do or who you are.

It may not be easy at first to stop taking things personally, but I can testify that life becomes so much easier, lighter and more joyful when you can. The good news is that you even don't have to do this the whole time to experience the peace it brings. In heated situations you will immediately feel the benefit. For me the consequence was that because of the good results I had in this one instance, I started applying it more and more to other events. In other words, it was no effort at all and became a more natural way of interacting with people.

Focus on your own path, stop comparing

One of the reasons we are suffering in life is that our wicked warriors compare our situation with those of other people.

For example,
- "They make more money than I do." Comparison: I'm being treated in a bad way.
- "They have a good-looking partner and I don't even have a partner." Comparison: Poor me, nobody wants to be with me.
- "They have a nicer car." Comparison: They must have sold drugs in order to be able to buy it. I can't afford such a car with my wage and I don't want be such a low life as them (but actually I'm VERY jealous of the car).

However, remember that everybody's path is different. Not everybody is here in this lifetime to learn the same lessons or to have the same experiences.
And, it may be they are triggered in a negative way by the things you deem positive.

For example, let's look at the above examples again, how may it be from their perspective:

- I received a raise and a promotion at work. Now I'm responsible for even more people. I don't know if I can handle this situation.
- In the beginning I really liked my partner. But now he is very possessive. I'd rather be single again.
- I just got a brand new car. I really like it. But I'm terrified that someone will make a scratch on it. It is parked on the street so I can't sleep at night. Every hour I look out the window to see if it's still there and make sure no one has touched it.

In other words, what may look as good, as positive or as an advantage to you, could be perceived by someone else as the opposite!

You never know what is going on in other people's minds or lives. You never know which thoughts they have picked, identified with and valued, so comparing is useless.

In the *Way of Mastery,* the following expression is used: "I don't know what my brother or sister needs." For me this is a good mantra to say inside my head and heart when meeting someone new or when having a conversation with a loved one. It's particularly helpful when I have been triggered or when I have noticed that I have been doing most of the talking.

When you let people off the hook and you're able to look at them with the mentality "I don't know what they need," you will become more open. Remember, they are just playing a role in your game, and they are just bringing gifts. Not only will you feel less like you're in attack mode, and thus lighter, you will also have more space to go to your own center. When you can ask questions and respond from your center, then you are immersed in love energy. Not only will you feel even lighter, but also will you bring that same 'lighter' energy to others. It's up to others to feel it, appreciate it and to accept the invitation to loosen their Phase 1 game. They may choose to do so or not. You don't have to do anything specifically. You don't have to explain anything to them or point out what is happening. Doing so may actually close the door again since their wicked warriors may feel they are being attacked.

Just keep what you see happening to yourself. Then, watch with amazement how your relationships will change. They'll change just because you decided to look at them differently. It is not a hard or difficult thing to do. It's just choosing to do something other than playing the Phase 1 game from the outpost.

Invitation 3: Look with wonder

Let's look again how judgment originates.

Let's look at the 'experience model' again:

1. There is a one large field of energy everything exists in.
2. All thoughts float around in this energy field. All thoughts are neutral and are available to everyone.
3. One of the wicked warriors picks out a thought and identifies with it: "This is MY thought."
4. Some of the thoughts are valued as 'true' and others as 'false'. As a consequence any behavior that is in line with what is perceived as true is 'right' and desirable, all other behavior is 'wrong' and despicable.
5. The longer we give our attention to a thought, the more it becomes a belief. The more important we deem a belief and the more we identify with it, the more intense our experiences with it will be.
6. Our experience is, the more the thoughts and beliefs that we have valued as 'true' are confirmed, the more relaxed we are. Our wicked warriors are at rest. The more that thought or belief is denied or the more the thought that we have valued as 'false' is triggered, the more stressed we are. The more stressed we are, the more active our wicked warriors are. They become active because they are looking for ways to attack/defend.
7. We react, verbally or physically (or we don't react and keep it to ourselves).

Step 4 is where judgment originates. The moment we label something as 'right' or 'wrong' we are judging. The height and severity of the judgment is created in step 5 and 6.

Now, there is something interesting happening with the 'false' thoughts and the ones that are opposite of 'true'. In step 3 there is identification with that thought and then that thought is kind of thrown away in step 4. I explicitly write 'kind of' thrown away, because if that were really be the case, it wouldn't do anything; there would be no trigger or reaction. It would be neutral.

What actually happens is, the responsibility for identifying with the thought is denied. We are thinking the thought, but we say it is not ours. We dissociate from the thought. When there is no responsibility for something, it becomes worthless. It can be discarded. So it is OK to attack it. It's small and worthless, so it is OK to be disrespectful. It won't matter.

For example, let's assume we have the thoughts "We are good people. Good people don't steal." They have been valued as 'true' and have become beliefs. The opposite would be "People who steal are bad. They are criminals. Criminals should be severely punished." Then we dissociate or separate from other people who are judged as bad. As a consequence it is only a small step to imprison people and to 'kick them out of society'.

At the same time, since we identified with that thought or belief in step 3, every time we judge or attack it, we hurt ourselves. Most of the time we are not aware of it, but we feel pain. The twisted Phase 1 trick is then that we think the pain comes from the 'bad stuff' ('false' thoughts or thoughts that are opposite to the 'true' ones), but actually it comes from our own judgment, projection or attack.

If we look at the example again: the person who believes, "People who steal are criminals" and who reads about a burglary, will feel angry. He thinks he has a 'negative' feeling because of the burglary, but actually it is because of his own judgment.

A rather easy first step to deal with this mechanism is to become aware of your actions and reactions (Step 7) and to postpone your normal reaction. The traditional advice to, 'count to 10 before reacting', is still very good advice! In this way you won't retaliate (or at least not immediately ☺). However, your emotions may still feel high. You still may feel the hurt.

We can also stop things sooner than Step 7 (reacting verbally or physically), before our emotions get too high. And it's a very good idea to do so. Why? When our emotional level is too high, it is often impossible to stop our reaction. It feels like it HAS to come out, like a volcano that can't be stopped from erupting.

Look with wonder

So let's focus on step 4 where we value our thoughts. Remember that everything is neutral. Also keep in mind that you don't know anyone's background or history. Remember that they are not out there to attack you, they are simply immersed in their own Phase 1 game.

When you start looking at all events and objects as neutral, you can become the witness: you just look at things, without labeling them as 'true' or 'false' (which prevents them from being labeled as 'right' or 'wrong'). They just 'are'.

Become like a child again. Look at the world in wonder. A child doesn't know what something is or what something is for. Children have to be taught the concept of 'right' and 'wrong'. Children constant ask their parents to explain the world to them.

For children the world is neutral. They look at it with wonder. It is only when names, labels and explanations are given, usually by their parents, that the world loses its neutrality or objectivity. When parents tell a child something is 'good' or 'bad' then it loses its innocence. One parent may tell a child that playing in mud puddles is 'bad', while another parent may encourage their child to explore puddles, mud and nature. Nature and puddles are neutral. It's how the child, or parent perceives them that alters or determines the child's thoughts and actions about a thing or experience. For example,

Example 1
- "Daddy, what is this?"
- Answer 1: "It's a stove. It is used to heat the house so we can all be warm."
- Answer 2: "It's a stove. You need to stay away from it, because you can burn yourself and have a lot of pain."

Example 2
- "Mommy, what is this?"
- Answer 1: "That is a bee. It makes honey. That is very yummy to put on a sandwich."
- Answer 2: "That is a bee. Stay away from it. It may sting you. That will hurt a lot."

So the invitation is: 'outsmart' your judgment by looking at the world with wonder. Do it both for the thoughts and beliefs you deem 'true' and the ones you deem 'false'. Do it for both the 'good', (answers 1) and the 'bad', (answers 2) ones. The fastest relief will come from looking at the 'bad stuff' as neutral, but if you really want to have more peace, joy and happiness, understand that the 'good stuff' also asks to be made neutral.

Although this last sentence may sound strange, it is actually more about releasing the attachment to the 'good stuff' than the 'good stuff' itself. It is about giving up the striving for the 'good stuff'. Why? Because it implicitly means that you want to avoid the 'bad stuff'. And you are then still playing the Phase 1 game.

What is interesting is that by giving up the striving and just letting it happen, there will be predominantly 'good stuff' in your life. The difference is that there will be no rejection of the 'bad stuff'. There will be no attack/defense game. So your general experience is more relaxed. Also when something 'negative' happens, you will be more relaxed.

Understanding the differences in values

In step 4 we have seen that we put a value on thoughts. To make things a bit more complex, there is also a personal hierarchy among our values.

For example, Frank has both the values 'family' and 'creativity' on his list. But he values 'family' more than 'creativity'. This means that in a situation where he needs to choose between them, he will choose 'family' over creativity. As a consequence he may choose a night with his parents over finishing painting the bathroom (which he identified as a creative project).

This is his personal preference, which is neutral. However, his values may be the reason for a discussion or a clash with other people. This happens when they have other values or another priority of those values.

For example, suppose Frank's partner Marie has the values 'safety' and 'listening' high on her list. She may be very upset that Frank goes to his parent's house leaving all his tools spread out in the bathroom. She may even be more upset when Frank leaves without talking about why he's leaving, or without his listening to her concerns. At the same time Frank doesn't have a clue why Marie is so mad. The reason he doesn't understand her anger is that the values 'safety' and 'listening' are very low on his list.

In order to understand someone else better, it may be a good idea to find out what your values are as well as what their values are. This will avoid many unnecessary fights and relax the wicked warriors.

The above example is a very simple one. Values don't only play a role between two individuals, they also affect families, teams at work, communities and sports teams. They play even a role on a higher level: cities, regions and countries.

An organization that specializes in helping individuals and groups get insights in values and understanding how to understand each other, is the Barrett Values Center.

For more information about them and instructions on how to get a free Personal Values Assessment, visit the free Library on the website of the book (**www.life-is-a-game.org**).

Invitation 4: Be aware of your identifications

In Invitation 3 we looked into how to avoid getting into the attack/defend game by choosing to look at the world with wonder. It was Step 4 from the 'experience model'.

Let's go a step further back.

Let's look at step 3. In this step we see how we identify with certain thoughts. Later on we expand our identification with other things:

- Objects: car, house, computer
- People: partner, children, friends (actual people like John, Mary, etc.)
- Places: city, region, country, continent
- Roles: child, parent, profession, employer/employee, partner, neighbor, friend

The moment we have identified with something, and we 'have' it, we possess it. Or at least we think we do ☺. And what happens automatically: the potential of 'loss' comes in the picture. Once we possess something, it can be lost. And in order to prevent this, it needs to be defended. That's where actually the wicked warriors step in, as the protectors of what could be lost.

Let's look at some examples.

Example 1

At the time when my book *How to REALLY use LinkedIn* was an international best seller, I used to identify myself with being a 'successful author and speaker' (identification with professional role).

Afterwards, when I looked closer at my success, I saw some associations with beliefs like: "A successful speaker doesn't pick up the office phone."

What was behind that thought? I dug deeper and found out: "A successful speaker has a team that works for him. If I pretend to be a successful speaker and people hear that I pick up the phone myself, they will think I'm a liar, that I'm a fraud. Then they will attack me."

The reality was, when I was the only person in the office I didn't pick up the phone. I'd rather have it go to voice mail so somebody else from the team could call back. That was the strategy of my wicked warriors to avoid being attacked because I was so identified with my role as 'successful speaker' and the thoughts I associated with that role. When I look back on it now, I think this situation is hilarious, but I was 'dead serious' about it at the time. That makes it even funnier when I look back ☺.

Example 2

In my partner relationships with women, I wanted to be a good boyfriend (role as partner). One of the thoughts I associated with the role of boyfriends is that they take care of their girlfriends. It sounds good, right?

But when I looked deeper into that association and what it meant for me (not for them!), I saw something odd. I thought that I must be available to them to cater to all their needs all the time. Without being aware of it, I stepped into the 'rescuer role' and pushed them into the 'victim role'.

Since we have many roles at the same time and many identifications with other things as well, it probably doesn't surprise you that such a role conflicted with another identification and value I held. I strongly identified with the value of freedom (including time for myself). However, I was also not aware of how strong that identification was, nor did I see the conflict that had arisen from two supposedly 'good' values.

So what happened? In the beginning of the relationship I was a perfect gentleman, always ready for my lady. After a while, I unconsciously started to blame her for taking up so much of my time and my freedom. Then the tension between those two identifications built up internally. The tension and resentment grew until I ended the relationship. That totally surprised her since she wasn't aware of my inner struggle. That same struggle with others also caused me to behave so differently and annoyingly that they ended the relationship. In other words, my wicked warriors started to attack. When they attacked, she could justify retaliating and I could be the victim. Funny how this works, isn't it ☺.

When roles (or other things we associate with) start to create conflict, that is the moment when the real mess starts. But since you are aware of this now, you can choose differently.

Invitation: look honestly at what you identify with.

1. Look at a role (or person, place, situation, etc.) you have identified with.
2. Think of what you value in this role.
   a. What is important to do, to have or to be in this role?
   b. What is important to avoid in this role?
   c. What are other associating thoughts?
3. Why are they so important? What can you gain or lose when they are, or are not, present or fulfilled?
4. What would happen if they were not present or fulfilled?
5. Is this really the truth? Would it really be a catastrophe? Would it affect who you REALLY are? Or is it the wicked warriors that feel threatened?

When you become more aware of how this works you may be shocked at what you discover about yourself, and what you feel embarrassed or ashamed about. At least I was embarrassed when I realized my identification with 'not picking up the phone' ☺. However, remember those feelings are just another Phase 1 trick to keep you in the outpost.

Be gentle with yourself. Praise yourself for having the courage to look at your identifications. Praise yourself for choosing differently. Praise yourself for choosing to start to play the love-based game instead of the fear-based game. Know that I'm cheering you on. Know that I'm applauding you. I know what it's like to look at identifications and be ashamed of them. But most of all I also know what lies beyond that choice: peace, joy and freedom. I know the rewards are big!

Invitation 5: Mind the patterns in your life

In Chapter 1 you read about the victim-persecutor-rescuer pattern/strategy.

This strategy is a shorter version of the drama triangle by Stephen Karman. It is a model that originates from Transactional Analysis. It's a very interesting field, so when you feel inspired, certainly delve deeper into it.

For the scope of this book and to keep things in the perspective of day-to-day application, I have found that the simple version from Chapter 1 works quite well.

There is the rather obvious perspective that when you attack someone you are the persecutor. The other perspective is that the one who is attacked will feel like a victim and will defend themselves. However, there are a few other situations that are less black and white or blatantly obvious. There are situations that we are usually not aware of that also trigger these roles.

- Situation A
  - You feel like a victim.
  - That makes the other person a persecutor. So you make him the persecutor, whether or not he wants to play this role.

- Situation B
  - You feel like a savior, a rescuer.
  - That makes the other person a victim. So you make him the victim, whether or not he wants to play this role.

What happens in both cases? The other person will resist playing this part, by attacking (when being perceived as the persecutor) or defending (when being perceived as the victim). And in this way, you will feel strengthened in your belief that they are exactly what you have perceived them to be. However, they act this way because **you** put them in this situation, **not because they ARE** a persecutor or victim.

For example,

Situation A:
- Step 1. Other person: "Can you do the dishes?" (neutral question)
- Step 2. You: "Why do I have to always do the dishes?" (reaction as a victim)
- Step 3. Other person: "Stop acting like such a baby." (attack)
- Step 4. You: "Why are you always so mean to me?" (counter attack)
- Step 5 and next steps: escalation by defending and attacking.

Situation B:

- Step 1. Other person: "Where do I find Word again on the computer? And those illustrations? I want to create the invitation for the party." (neutral question)
- Step 2. You: "Let me do it. It will only take me 10 minutes, and it will take you several hours." (reaction as a rescuer)
- Step 3. Other person: "Several hours? I'm not a complete idiot. Don't belittle me like that." (defense and attack)
- Step 4. You: "Then do it yourself. I even don't want to help you anymore." (counter attack)
- Step 5 and next steps: escalation by attacking and defending.

Most of the times, these situations happen because of the underlying, subconscious victim-persecutor/rescuer pattern. And we get into fights without even knowing what the cause was. Being aware of when you are in such a pattern or when such situations arise is a first step to release the pattern. To release both yourself and the other person/people involved in it from the (recurring) patterns. To start shifting this, remember that every event is neutral. It is only our wicked warriors that are vigilant and on the look out for possible attacks.

So, next time you find yourself in a situation as above, consider approaching it this way:

When you feel your response coming up in step 2, see if you can stop yourself from reacting. Remember that you can choose differently. You can look at all events as neutral.

When you find yourself in step 4 (when you were not aware of it happening in step 2), remember you can still choose differently. Everybody is expressing love or asking for love. When you are aware of the 'battle' that has begun, it is just a reminder that you have chosen to identify with your outpost instead of your centered self.

That's actually what happened in the example of me being triggered about 'me space' in the house.

These are the steps you can take:
1. You realize that you are in a 'battle'.
2. If the battle has already heated up, ask to be excused for a minute (a time-out).
3. You choose to go from the outpost to the center.
4. You may feel the connection with your Higher Self, but that is not even necessary. Being removed from the outpost is mostly enough to feel your own strength again.
5. Say in your mind, "I choose to have a good relationship with this person. I want both of us to be happy. The event is neutral. It is only fear-based energy

that has come up between us. The other person is not the cause, only the trigger."

6. If you are really centered, most of the time you will be inspired to speak the right words.

If you don't find the right words in step 6, these are a few approaches you could take:

- Whether you don't know exactly what happened or you do know what happened, but don't want to share it, you can still say, "I'm sorry for my reaction. I just realized that I was triggered. I wasn't triggered because of you, but what happened between us triggered something in me from my past. Can you repeat your question again please?"
- If you don't know what exactly happened, but are open to exploring it, you or the other person may choose to explore what happened with you in the past and try to find out what it was. However, that is not always necessary or possible.
- If you do know what happened and want to share it you can choose to do so: "I'm sorry for my reaction. I just realized that I was triggered. Not because of you, but what happened between us triggered something in me from my past. It was exactly how my father acted when I was a child and it always made me feel not good enough."

Being honest and vulnerable is very, very powerful. It also invites the other person to leave his Phase 1 game and move to his center. I can personally testify that 'miracles' have happened in this way!

Caution: this only works when you are doing this from your center. Otherwise you create another victim-rescuer/persecutor cycle. When you feel like a victim, you will push the other person into a savior/rescuer role.

Invitation: become aware of the victim-rescuer/persecutor patterns in your life and decide to choose differently. You will experience how your life becomes lighter, more peaceful and more joyous!

Invitation 6: Put yourself first

As explained before, you came here on this planet and into this three-dimensional world to play a game, the human game.

Other people, objects, places, situations are here to help you play the game. It may not look that way, and other people may not be consciously aware of their role in your life, but that's because the game needs this kind of complexity to be interesting enough to be played.

Let's take one of the first computer games ever invented as an example. The game is called Pong. When playing Pong the only thing you saw on the screen was a line on the left hand side, a line on the right hand side, and a dot in the middle. The goal of the game was to use the line on your side as a paddle or barrier for the dot (you could call it a 'ball'). The goal was to reflect or block the ball in a way that the other person would not be able to catch it when it 'bounced' back to them. In other words, the game was a great deal like table tennis (or ping pong), only on a computer. If you had to play this game day in, day out, you would eventually get very good, but be very bored as well. That's why computer games have evolved greatly. They've become much more complex, with several levels, storylines or quests that keep them interesting. The same thing applies to the human game: it needs to be complex enough to remain interesting!

Now, since your life is **your** game you can, or even need to, put yourself first.

"But what about other people then? Especially my old mother and my handicapped son who can't live without me. They can't survive without me. And what about all those hungry children in Africa? I need to rescue them as well!" you may say.

Actually, it may be true that you may be of help to them. But what happens most of the time is that those are Phase 1 games in the form of victim-rescuer/persecutor patterns.

To truly be of help to anyone, you have to put yourself first. It is like the instructions in the airplane: when the cabin pressure is lost, parents need to put on their oxygen mask first before helping their children put their own masks on. If they first help their children, they may pass out before being able to put on their own oxygen mask. When the parent is passed out because they tended to others first, then they are of no help to anyone for the things that follow.

I hope this example also shows that choosing for yourself first doesn't mean that you are choosing against someone else. On the contrary; when we put ourselves first, when we make sure that our cup is full, we can be of better assistance to others because we actually have more to share with them.

"Is this not egoistic (with a negative connotation)?" you might ask. Well, yes and no. It depends how you define *egoism*. If you look at egoism from the Phase 1 game point of view, you might perceive it as negative. Then someone is putting himself first by attacking others. So it is at the cost of others. That is not what we are talking about here. When playing the Phase 2 or 3 game putting yourself first won't be at the expense of somebody else. Egoism then becomes a very positive word.

So how does this relate to what we are talking about in this book?

It is of fundamental importance that you first find your center, and preferably the connection with your Higher Self, before taking any action. That's the only way to keep out of the Phase 1 games. It's also the only way you can really be of help to someone else. The greatest help you can give someone is to show them that the solution is in the center, not in the outpost with the warlike wicked warriors. By BE-ing in your center (and not DO-ing anything), you inspire other people to also look for their center.

If you are in your center and are consciously connected with your Higher Self, and if you feel moved or inspired to take care of your old mother, handicapped son or starving children in Africa, please do so. Then your actions are 'inspired actions' in a love-based game! Do it because it is your way to extend love, to shine and to radiate your beauty. Not because you're dredging up old rescuer patterns in order to get approval or avoid rejection. Those old patterns only make others into victims.

Invitation 7: Interact with compassion

When you realize that almost everybody is still playing the Phase 1 game (some of us play it all the time, others just play it once in a while), and they are not out to get you, but are dealing with their own fears, you can start looking at them in a different way.

When you are centered yourself, you can look at the world in a different way. You can start to look with compassion and with love.

A sentence from *A Course in Miracles* that helps a lot is, "Everything is an expression of love or a cry for love." So when someone is not expressing love, they are asking for love. They are asking for assistance so they can release themselves from the Phase 1 game.

Everybody can provide this help, provided that they are not immersed in their own Phase 1 game. Otherwise you may end up in the victim-rescuer/persecutor trap.

Another pitfall is that you may mix up being empathic with being sympathetic.

Let me explain.

When you are sympathetic:

- You may fall into the victim-rescuer/persecutor trap.
- Your own old pains or fears can be triggered. As a result, you are focusing on yourself and not on the other person anymore.
- If you are very sensitive, you may take over energies that are not yours, feel overwhelmed and become totally drained during or after the conversation.

Being empathic means being compassionate. You are there for the other person, you are with them, but only from a witness perspective. You are not joining them in their suffering. The more centered you are and the more you are connected to your Higher Self, the easier it is to be in this empathic/compassionate position. And the better you can help others.

A note of caution: when you are empathic and not sympathetic, sometimes people may accuse you of being cold or distant. What is happening then is a combination of:
- Them being totally immersed in their own Phase 1 game.
- Them not being able to find someone who is willing to play the game of attack/defense with.
- You choosing NOT to play the Phase 1 game, but also not totally being in your center yet.

Having others accusing you of being cold or distant is yet another trick of the wicked warriors. It is their attempt to get you to join them in playing the Phase 1 game. By acting like a victim they want to make you the rescuer. When you don't take up this role, they feel the only way to deal with this is to attack you. They do this by accusing you of being cold. This is an attempt to weaken your position, to prod you, to get you from your center to your outpost where you can be the rescuer (again).

If you feel that you can't take the pressure because you are not centered enough, it is good to take a time-out. Remove yourself mentally, or even physically, from the situation. You can, for example, go to the bathroom, or excuse yourself to get some fresh air, or a glass of water so you can get more centered or more connected. Remember that you can only give real help to someone when you are in your center. You can only help when they have asked for help, so it's not unsolicited advice and therefore placing them in a victim role. The real help they need, is to get out of the Phase 1 game. And you can only inspire them to do so by being centered yourself. If you don't feel strong enough yet to come back after the time-out, then it is a good idea to remove yourself physically from the situation for a longer time. "I don't think I'm ready to discuss this now. Let's continue this later." Yes, you will get more screaming, shouting, accusing and maybe even swearing. The more they are identified with their outpost, the more intense this can be. It may be hard for you to keep your mouth shut and go away, but it's the only thing you can do. Red-hot wicked warriors won't listen to any advice anyway.

What helps when choosing to be compassionate is to remember:
- All events are neutral.
- You don't know the background or history of someone.
- You don't know which monsters they are dealing with (you may even never have heard of such monsters).
- Everything is an expression of Love or a call for Love. If they are not expressing Love, they are looking for It. Who can be mad at someone who is just looking for love? How do you answer a call for love? With love, right?
- You don't need to give answers. Just by being in your center (and if possible being connected to your Higher Self) you can inspire them to look at things differently as well.
- You don't have to *do* anything, you just can *be*.

Invitation 8: Forgive others and especially yourself

A very strong way to loosen up the power of the wicked warriors so they can be reprogrammed as your loving helpers, is to forgive.

When we are still fully immersed in the Phase 1 game, forgiving looks like this:
- That person attacked me.
- I feel like a victim.
- I will forgive her (but I won't forget).
- This makes me the better person and her the wrong one. By blaming her, I make myself stronger and larger. This makes me feel better about myself so I can go on with my life.
- I may have forgiven, but I haven't forgotten it because I need to be vigilant for future attacks. I have already chosen which game to play next time: "Poor me, don't do it again" (being the victim), "Poor thing, it's not her fault" (rescuer) or "I will make sure that I will deal the first blow," (being the persecutor).

This is actually not forgiving at all. It is making the current event a cease-fire so one can go on with their life.

It takes some awareness to look at forgiveness in another way. The good news is that since you are reading this part of the book awareness is already present. So you don't have to do anything anymore. Isn't that great? ☺

What does real forgiving look like?

It has actually two levels:
1. Forgiving the other person and asking for forgiveness
2. Forgiving yourself

Forgiving the other person and asking for forgiveness

It helps to keep this in mind:
- All events are neutral.
- I don't know the background or history of the other person.
- Everything is an expression of Love or a call for Love.
- They are not out there to get me. They are stuck in their own Phase 1 game.
- This quote may help as well: "Forgiving is releasing the hope it could have been different."

Then you can say in silence, "I forgive that this has happened."

A very simple process that helped me a lot with forgiveness is *Ho'oponopono*. It is a four-step process of forgiveness. It is originally from Hawaii. It came on my path via other people using it in their workshops and books like Zero Limits (By Joe Vitale and Ihaleakala Hew Len).

What are the four steps or four sentences?

1. I'm sorry.
2. Please forgive me.
3. I love you.
4. Thank you.

In its simplest form you can use it like this: you visualize the person you have a conflict with and then, in silence say those four sentences a few times in a row.

What happens most of the time is you feel milder and more compassionate towards the other people involved. It becomes easier to step out of the Phase 1 game and go to your center.

After you've been doing this for a while, you may want to start playing with it a little more. You may want to change the order of the sentences if that feels more natural to you.

For example Gwendolyn always starts with "I love you," because she feels the heart energy streaming through, which is for her the foundation for the rest of the statements. I like to start with "I'm sorry," because I feel it lowers resistance, providing a willingness to open up to hear the other three sentences. But in the end it doesn't matter, because the four sentences are used anyway (and besides that, even the exact sentences don't matter ☺. If you find alternatives that feel better to you, please use them).

And you can also play in other ways with the sentences. For example, I use them in this way:

Example A:

1. Gwendolyn, I'm sorry that I reacted defensively, it was a trigger from my past.
2. Please forgive me.
3. I love you.
4. Thank you.

Example B:

1. Dear customer, I'm sorry.
2. Please forgive me for pressuring you to sign the contract.
3. I love you.
4. Thank you.

Example C:

1. Dear landlord, I'm sorry that I felt like a victim, making you the persecutor (or: … that I perceived you as a persecutor).
2. Please forgive me.
3. I love you.
4. Thank you.

If your partner or colleague is also reading this (part of the) book, you can also say those sentences out loud to each other. Then it becomes even more powerful! I invite you to play with it. Make them your own sentences.

More tips, examples, explanations and background about Ho'oponopono can be found in the free library on the website.

Forgiving yourself

While the process of forgiving others is already a very powerful process, and an excellent way of moving from the outpost to the center, it is just a first step. It is still in the realm of the Phase 1 game with its wicked warriors.

What I have found to be one of the most profound, and the easiest ways to release the wicked warriors from their heavy duty and to connect with my Higher Self is to forgive myself.

"Forgive yourself of what?" you may ask.

Forgive myself of playing the Phase 1 game instead of the Joyful Game of Life.

When I use Ho'oponopono again, it may look like this:

1. Dear Higher Self, I'm sorry that I got caught up in playing the Phase 1 game.
2. Please forgive me for being distracted from playing the Joyful Game of Life.
3. I love you.
4. Thank you for unconditionally loving me.

In this way I feel centered and connected in just a few seconds.

Again, be creative with it. Make your own sentences. The most important part is that you feel what they do to you. Borrow other people's sentences, but only if they feel right to you.

Invitation 9: Be totally honest

One of the most powerful invitations to accept is to be totally honest. I can personally testify that this is true. Many things in my life have turned around very quickly once I started to look deeply inside myself, and to be honest about everything (or at least about the things that have showed themselves so far ☺). It's not an easy invitation to begin with, since the wicked warriors will do everything they can to have you do something else. They will scream and shout in your head, they will try to convince you with logical arguments not to go this route.

Why? Because they know that if you start going this route, they will lose their power over you. Because they are so full of fear they cannot think of anything else. This is simply how they react. But what you can keep in mind is that you don't want to get rid of the wicked warriors, you just want to give them another role. You want to reprogram the robots from fear-based wicked warriors into love-based merry minstrels. However, to be able to do that, the best thing to do is to move from the outpost to your center. Only then will most people be strong enough to make that choice. When you are in the outpost with the wicked warriors, the noise they make is so loud that you can't see or think of anything else.

One of the best ways to move to your center is to be honest about anything that happens in your life. This also requires some vulnerability. If you are still in or close to the outpost, you will hear the wicked warriors scream: "No, not vulnerability. They will attack you and destroy you. Don't go that route. Come with us. We will look out for danger and once we see it, we will defend you so they can't attack you. We will help you to not get hurt!" This can be a very tempting call, especially if you have been hurt a lot in your life.

However, what you will experience when having more moments of honesty in which you are vulnerable is that you will become invulnerable. What will happen is that people who played the attack/defense game with you, will stop doing that. You could say that being vulnerable is disarming. Being vulnerable takes away your adversaries' ammunition.

For example, there was a moment with the team at Networking Coach that we had invested a lot of money in a project. The project didn't go through and we lost a lot of money. Our cash flow position was very bad. It was the end of Spring. In the training industry the Summer period is the period with smaller revenues because most companies don't organize training courses then.

As a consequence there was not enough money to pay the team. I felt very sad, mad, frustrated and powerless. I had always been the one with the vision, solutions and ideas, but this time I didn't have any. I felt like I was letting everybody down.

But there was no other option than to be very honest and tell them what was going on.

With all the courage I could find I told them about the situation. Because I had always been rather open about the financial situation, it was not a real shock to them. But instead of being mad at me or projecting frustration, they came up with a solution themselves: everybody was prepared to work at half fee (note: they were all self-employed, there were no employees). So, for the next couple of months, until the situation got better, they worked for half their fees. In other words: by being honest, I felt accepted and a heavy weight fell from my shoulders. And moreover, a solution was presented that I hadn't thought of.

So I can only invite you to be honest. It really pays off! Be warned though! The fear-based energy is a strong one ☺. Always be vigilant about whether you are really being honest and vulnerable, or whether you are playing the Phase 1 game. Playing the victim game can look like being vulnerable (and you may expose yourself a lot), but it is still about fear-based energy, not about what is really going on.

Actually, the difference in being 'really vulnerable' and being 'fake vulnerable' (Phase 1) is in whether you are being honest or not. If you really go inside, look at your monster and talk about it, then people will feel it is true honesty. When you talk about something that is not a 'good quality', like "I'm an alcoholic," but it is something you identify with, it is not true honesty.

The difference may be subtle, but you will feel it when you pay attention to your intuition or when you ask questions. When it is about a monster, at first people can't talk about it at all. It is too bad and too big. It can't be spoken of. But when they have looked at it, it kind of deflates. It turns into a teddy bear. Once this has happened, people can't believe they were so afraid. And actually there is nothing more to talk about. The monster is gone.

When people identify with something, they can talk for hours about it. Even when they feel (or seem) embarrassed about it. When they are identified with it, it has value to them. The value can be that it provides them with a way to play the victim-persecutor/rescuer game. As long as they are not willing to look at what is really behind this identification, as long as they are not willing to look at the real monster, they will continue this game. Or they may trade it for another game, for example from being addicted to alcohol to being addicted to smoking, sex, shopping or food.

So how do you start with being totally honest?

First, you may want to start with small things, and smaller monsters. Just do it on your own. Then you can move on to bigger monsters. Although it is scarier to have other people involved ("they may judge me"), they may be a great help.

Sometimes the larger monsters seem so overwhelming that you feel like you can't face them alone. That is just exactly how you set this up when planning your current human game as a non-physical being, however, some assistance may be welcome. The best approach to request assistance from a friend in this matter is this: ask them if they can just be present. Tell them they don't have to do anything, but that you just want them to be present and listen to you. Although it may sound strange to take this approach, your friend will be honored to do so and also be relieved that he doesn't have to provide the solution.

For example, one of my monsters (fears) was that when this book was not complete, when it didn't contain all the tools and the methods and when it was not perfect, it wouldn't be appealing enough to the readers. So I asked Gwendolyn: "I have a monster and I want to share it with you. This will help me to really look at it. It will help me to not put it aside to be dealt with later (or never ☺). Will you just be here with me and listen to me? You don't have to do or say anything." She gladly agreed and in no time the monster was seen, deflated and its power was gone. Although Gwendolyn didn't do anything, I felt her love and support. That was enough, not only to 'neutralize' the monster, but also turn it into a teddy bear. In this case the teddy bear was the insight that by sharing my fears with you, the reader, it would make this book more powerful than anything else. So that's what I did. You will find my fears in Chapter 3. Besides that, there was also the insight that this book didn't have to be complete; that there are other ways to share additional knowledge. In a very practical way this meant that I took the decision to share additional information in the Library on the website of the book and to open up the possibility of creating additional books (or a series) about topics that didn't find a spot in this book.

So be honest. Although you may think it will cause rejection (I thought that Gwendolyn would think less of me, because I was not 100% certain about myself), the opposite almost always happens: people will accept you more for who you are. Or maybe they won't be totally accepting, but at least the rejection will be gone. Remember, you are playing *your* game. You are being honest for yourself, not for others. Don't make it another Phase 1 game where you only try to be honest to receive approval from others or avoid rejection.

Invitation: be honest with yourself. Be totally brutally honest with yourself. It is one of the most liberating things you can do in your life! Enjoy it!

Invitation 10: Be aware of your input and output

Output: your own language

Perhaps this is one of the easiest invitations to begin with: become aware of the language you are using. By using less war-like language and more harmonious words, you will have less conflict with other people and you will start floating from the outpost towards the center. With *easier* I mean, if you are not yet ready to start going deeper inside yourself, using other words may be an easier way to start the process.

However, since our language patterns are mostly wired in our brain from consistent use, this could be difficult without someone else's help. You can ask your partner, a friend or a colleague to help you become aware of certain fear-based words. Fear-based words are more focused on attacking and defending than on creating harmony.

What are some of the words to look out for?

All war-like words

For example, attack, defense, destroy, annihilate, offense, retreat, assault, protect, aggressive, fortify, guard, shield, trenches, weapons, ammunition, etc.

Especially in corporate environments and in sports this kind of language is used:
- Corporate environments:
    o "We have to arm ourselves for the next quarter."
    o "We have to defend our market share."
    o "Let's pull the trigger on this issue."
    o "We have to attack a specific target group."
- Sports:
    o Most sports talk about offense and defense. There are also many offensive and defensive strategies in any sports.
    o "We have them by the throat."
    o "That shot was the final blow for the team. It felt like an execution."
    o "We have to crush the enemy."

Pay attention to these words and how you use them. If you don't use these phrases, think about the ones you do use that could be considered war-like. Ask for help if your words and phrases are blind spots to you.

The word 'But'

Have you actually paid attention to what happens when you or someone else uses the word 'but' in a sentence?

"I appreciated you doing the dishes yesterday, but how could you forget to use the vacuum cleaner? I put it right in front of the door."

Two things are happening in this specific sentence:
1. The word 'but' wipes out everything that precedes it. It is like a verbal eraser. People don't remember the words before 'but' anymore. The word 'but' is like a red flag: this is what you are doing wrong and because of that reason I'm rejecting you or attacking you.
2. If you read this sentence out loud, like if you were saying it yourself to someone, can you notice how it builds up to the 'but'? We are so trained in how people do this, that we are already anticipating the 'but' coming when people seem to be praising us. In other words, we are already preparing for the rejection or attack. And, when we are already in defensive mode, we are no longer listening to what the message or the intention behind the message is. We are only focused on our defense.

The result of the sentence above is not that the person feels good. It's that the other person feels attacked and shouts something like: "I can never do anything that is good enough for you! I'm leaving." And the vicious fear-based cycle has started once again.

The words 'Yes, but'

A variation on 'but' is 'yes, but'. It actually works the same way.

Both 'but' and 'yes, but' are signs that we are fighting to be right. The question many authors and coaches ask is, "Would you rather be right or be happy?" Many people protest: "When I'm right, I'm right. I won't give it up." However, many times we're not fighting for the content. The 'but', or the 'yes, but' are patterns of fighting for dominance. They are about a victim-persecutor pattern.

What you will see happening is that when you are in your center and are having conversations with people, what is 'right' (whether it is your opinion or the other person's opinion) will be what the outcome of the conversation is. Or, something better will come up. You will not only keep the relationship harmonious, you'll also feel good during the discussion because you are in your center and not in the stressful outpost. Using 'but' or 'yes, but' hardly ever gets us out of the outpost and into our center. As a consequence the results from our conversations will be less than optimal (to put it nicely ☺).

Exaggerations

These are words like ever, never, always, etc.

When you use words like these, people will go in defensive mode. They will perceive those words as not reflecting the truth, but rather as an attack.

Example: when you are frustrated that you had to take the garbage cans out again instead of your partner (whose chore it is):
- You: "You never put the garbage outside."
- Your partner: "Never? I did it 3 weeks ago."
- You: "And before? I always have to do your chores."
- Your partner: "The only thing you always do, is exaggerate."
- And the vicious fear-based game has started once again.

The words 'Should, ought, must, need'

These are words to pay attention to, especially in your self-talk. I think it is obvious when you tell someone, "You must do the dishes," that they will go into defensive mode. For me those words, 'should, ought, must, need' have been red flags prompting me to battle: "How dare they command me. We shall see about what is actually going to happen." Or in other words: I was not only in defensive mode, but also in counter attack mode. Neither were good for my stress levels or for the relationship, that's for sure ☺. Although it may be obvious what kinds of emotions and responses these words can cause between people, what may be less obvious is the burden we put on ourselves when we use them in our self-talk.

When I became aware of how many times a day I said to myself (or to others about myself): "I **must** call Mr. Johnson. I **need** to read all my emails. I **should** write a new blog post," it was clear how much stress I was putting on myself. The reason all this was happening was because the wicked warriors believed that I wouldn't be attacked or criticized by others only if I worked hard.

"How can I do this differently?" you may ask. One tip is to use the word 'choose' instead of 'must, need, should, ought'. It then also becomes clear of what would give you energy and what not.

For example,
- "I choose to call Mr. Johnson." Well, I always like talking to him. The conversations are fun most of the time.
- "I choose to read all my emails." Pfff, that is an energy drain now. I choose to do it later so I can do something that gives me energy.
- "I choose to write a new blog post." Yes, I feel inspired right now. Let's do that, I already feel energized just thinking about it.

Nonviolent communication

If you want to go a step further and really focus on how you communicate, a process that I recommend is that of 'Nonviolent Communication' by Marshall Rosenberg. Other people have called it 'Connective Communication', to get the war-like word 'violent' out of the title.

In the Library on the website (**www.life-is-a-game.org**) you will find the model and some examples.

Your input: mind what you read, listen to and watch

This invitation is a very pragmatic one.

You are invited to be very aware of what you read, listen to, and watch.

Since most of the people in the world are still playing the Phase 1 game, this is what the prevailing or dominant game is. As a consequence mass media are immersed in the same energy and the same game. That is not a good or a bad thing, it is just a logical consequence. When more people are centered and are playing the love-based game, that too will be reflected in mass media as well. Actually there are already more websites, blogs and magazines than ever before that focus on love-based energy. They are on the rise and I look forward to the day that they achieve mass media status. If you choose to relax the wicked warriors, it is also wise to have the least fear-based energy input as possible in your life.

What helped me decrease the amount of fear-based energy in my life was to stop watching television, listening to the radio and reading newspapers. Or at least stop or limit the news, background programs regarding the news, and reality shows. These are programs that reflect the current energy of the masses, and as a consequence promote fear-based energy. Again, there is nothing good or bad about it, it just is.

"But what if I miss something?" you may ask.

I invite you to examine this question. And go very deep. Is there really anything that you need to know in the news? Is there anything you need to know in order to survive or prevent your physical body from being hurt? Or look at it from the other side: is there enough in the news that inspires and uplifts you (after your energy has been drained by all the 'negative' news) that truly makes it worth watching?

The same applies to social media. Are the people you are connected to more focused on fear-based energy or love-based energy? What are they posting and what are they sharing from other sources? How does that information make you feel? Is it lifting you up or pulling you down? Maybe it is time to block or remove some friends or contacts.

"But won't I miss information that is *really* important to me if I stop my 'news intake' and limit my friends and contacts on social media?" you may ask.

Any information that is really important for you, will find its way to you. One way or the other. I have been living like this for over seven years now and I can guarantee you that it works. I can understand that you still may be hesitant to do this. So I invite you to be very conscious in the next weeks. When you watch, read or listen to the news, pay attention to how it makes you feel. And write down what you heard that was actually relevant to you. In that way your wicked warriors have some reassurance that they will survive without it ☺.

People you associate with

One task that you may find harder than avoiding news and defriending people on Facebook, is to consciously look at who you interact with.

There is a saying: "You are the average of the five people you interact with the most." Whether or not that is true, it is still very worthwhile to look at the people who are close to you, and with whom you interact with a lot. If they are fully immersed in the Phase 1 game, they may be a big influence. They may drag you back in the Phase 1 game every time you want to choose differently.

How to deal with this situation?

First, the most important factor is that you are aware of what is happening. If you are aware that there are Phase 1 games at play, it becomes easier to not instantly react. When you don't counter attack, you won't feed the Phase 1 energy. Next, you may want to more consciously choose whom you spend your time with, and how much time you spend with them. The consequence could be that some of your friends or family members will fade out of your life. After a while, when you are more consciously aware of the Phase 1 game and you have learned to relax your own wicked warriors, you can start living more from your center.

What will happen then? First, you will notice that the people who annoyed or attacked you in the past, won't do that anymore (or they'll do it much less). Secondly, because of your center-based living, you may be an inspiration to them to also leave their outpost and abandon the Phase 1 game. People who faded out of your life before, may suddenly be very close to you again, but the energy between the two of you will be very different. There will be much more harmony, peace and joy!

Extra Invitation

Now, probably you have learned about some of the 'Invitations' from this chapter in other books or courses. What was missing for me in most of those courses was both the larger perspective of the human game, and the difference between the fear-based game of Phase 1 and the love-based game of Phase 2 and 3. Without that perspective I felt when I didn't follow the invitations I was not a good person. My wicked warriors were the ones feeling the pressure. They were the ones wanting me to keep playing their game.

However, now I understand that the 'Invitations' are ways to relax the wicked warriors. I don't have to be perfect in applying the 'Invitations'. Just applying them from time to time already helps relax the wicked warriors so I can float to the center.

You may not like the Phase 1 game. Like many people you may despise it and be mad at it. But that's actually another trick of the same wicked warriors ☺. It's only when you can embrace them that they will lose their attack/defense power and be transformed into merry minstrels. However, you can only embrace something that is smaller than you.

It's like a two person air mattress; when it is inflated it is rather hard to pick it up and move around when you don't have help. But when it is deflated it is easy to move by yourself. The same applies to the wicked warriors; as long as they are inflated, it is very hard to do anything with them. So you'd better deflate them first. The 'Invitations' from this chapter will help you with that.

If you still are mad at the Phase 1 game, look at it like an engineer looks at an engine: full of wonder at how the engine is constructed, full of admiration at its complexity, and full of awe at how everything fits together. The engineer doesn't judge the engine. It just is. My invitation to you is to look at the Phase 1 game like the engineer looks at the engine: full of wonder at how the game is constructed, full of admiration at its complexity and full of awe at how everything fits together. Look at it with mildness and compassion. When the wicked warriors are deflated, embrace them and invite them to join you in playing another game: the love-based game.

Chapter 3: Tools and Techniques

Sometimes there will be a situation where you need an immediate change. You may need an immediate release from the fear-based energy so you can be in your center (or at least out of your outpost) for some critical reason. Once you are in your center, you can look at the situation around you more clearly and objectively. You can even consciously connect with your Higher Self. In any case, you will receive more and better solutions from your center.

In order to assist you in getting an immediate release I have gathered a few techniques that are rather simple. They can be applied immediately and with no help from someone else.

However, if you have the opportunity to have someone you trust, be present with you when you apply the techniques, do so. It may be very beneficial. First of all, if they are centered, they will be able to invite you to come out of your outpost and float towards your center simply by being. They don't have to do anything. Besides that, they may offer you another way of looking at things or observe your blind spots and share them with you. However, if this person is part of the situation, or they are also in their outpost, playing the Phase 1 game (in many cases a subtle victim-rescuer game), it may be wise to do it alone. Remember you want to get out of the outpost now, so you don't need someone else confirming your fear-based thoughts in that moment. You need someone who is centered or otherwise it's better to do it by yourself.

If you could use more professional help, there is a directory of coaches, therapists, facilitators and healers on the website. Not only are they more neutral (and not feeding your fear-based thoughts nor playing the victim-rescuer game), but they also are more skilled in the basic techniques and tools, as well as additional tactics. They also have more experience in using a variety of tools and a combination of tools.

The models, exercises, tools and techniques in this chapter are a mix of immediate help and longer-term support. The ones with immediate results are designed to get you from a high emotional state to a lower one (and even to your center). Once you are a little less overwhelmed, you can use one or more of the techniques to gain more insights into the situation. Once you've done that, you can transform your monsters into teddy bears.

Note: in the book you will find a basic explanation of each tool or technique. Not everybody has the same preferences for tools and techniques. That's why there are several different approaches presented. To keep the book within reasonable length, extra techniques and tools, more background information, exercises, video clips and tips can be found in the *Library* on the website.

Immediate relief

Breathing

When people are overwhelmed or are suffering from too much stress, they breathe more shallowly. It's an old survival technique to prepare us to fight or flee.

So, the easiest way to get some relief when you're stressed and anxious is to start breathing more deeply. You will feel a deep breathing will relax you almost immediately.

A simple breathing exercise is the Sama Vritti (or 'Equal Breathing'). The focus of this exercise is to calm the nervous system, increase focus and reduce stress.

How to do it?

- Inhale for 4 counts.
- Then exhale for 4 counts.

Do them all through the nose.

Note: besides being effective in 'emergency' situations where a monster is overwhelming you, you can also do this before going to bed. If you have trouble falling asleep this breathing technique can help to take your mind of thoughts that keep running through your mind and are distracting you. This breathing technique can also help refocus your mind from anything else that may be distracting you from sleeping. If you wake up in the middle of the night and can't fall back to sleep, this will help you settle right back down almost immediately.

When you combine this with voice work (which may include singing), you may get even better results. At least that is what I have experienced ☺. There are several courses that may help you with that. In the meantime you can already start breathing more deeply.

Flower Remedies

For a definition I refer to the Collins Dictionary: *"Flower remedies are an alternative cure consisting of a distillation from various flowers, designed to counteract negative states of mind and restore emotional balance."*

In other words, they are perfect for handling the roaring wicked warriors ☺.

I have had many good results with them myself for different emotions and different 'monsters'. Flower remedies work both in the short and longer term.

The ones for immediate relief are:

- Rescue Remedy from Bach Flower Remedies Ltd
- Terra from Healing Herbs, Bach Flower Remedies

You will notice that after taking a few drops of them, you will feel calmer (for some people this works almost instantaneously, for others it can take some more time). It's always good to carry a vial with you for yourself or a friend. I always keep a vial at home and in the car.

Sprays

Flower remedies are also available as a spray. I use them to energetically cleanse a room. For example when I stay in a hotel I use the spray to neutralize the energy of the people who stayed there before me so I'm not triggered by that energy. I have also been using them before starting a workshop to cleanse the room's energy. Many times training rooms are used by many different people day in, day out. It was very interesting to see how participants (most of the time sales people and recruiters from industries like audit, banking/insurance, energy, ICT, law and telecom) became calmer once I started using these sprays, even when they weren't aware I'd used them!

Where to get them?

You can buy them online (see the Library on the website for details), however, going to a specialized shop or therapist will help you select the best sprays for your situation.

A good shop in Belgium is 'Het Vliegend Konijn': **www.hetvliegendkonijn.be** (disclaimer: it's Gwendolyn's shop, but I think you will forgive my biased opinion here ☺).

Movement

The word 'emotion' comes from the Latin 'emovere' (which means to move out or move through). However, when we are overwhelmed, most of the time we are also kind of paralyzed. By 'breaking' this paralyzed state by moving the body, things can get flowing again. Or in other words, by moving our body, we can help the feeling 'move out' or 'move through' us.

These are just a few examples of what you can do when this happens:

- Go for a short walk (or a long one like the Camino de Santiago de Compostela)
- Jog in a beautiful place
- Walk your dog
- Dance (in your living room, at a party or in a dance class)
- Jump on a (small) trampoline
- Any kind of sports activity
- Get your body moving in a way you enjoy

There are other ways to change your 'state' and hence get the feelings to move through your body instead of storing them (and getting stuck with them).

- Get a massage
- Go to a sauna
- Laugh
- Smile

Distraction

Sometimes all you need to get out of the Phase 1 game is to remove yourself from the situation in one way or the other.

A truly simple way to remove yourself is to simply distract yourself.

These are some examples of how to distract yourself:

- Read a book that inspires you (for me the books from *The Way of Mastery* series have this effect)
- Listen to music that makes your heart sing
- Pet your cat or dog, or watch your fish if you have an aquarium
- Take a nice shower or a hot bath
- Go for a drive in your car, or ride your bike

- Go to events where people who are in their center are likely to be
- Cook or bake something
- Create something with your hands: painting, sculpting, building
- Do anything else that you like

Have you noticed how many inspiring ideas or solutions you get under the shower or in the car? I do ☺.

The reason is that in these situations we are not focused so much on our worries. We are not in our outpost, but more in our center (without even knowing it). When we're more in our center, deliberately or not, it is easy for our Higher Self to feed us an inspiring thought or idea.

Again, the above list contains only some examples. Use your intuition or your feelings to determine what the right actions are for you.

Extra benefit

When you are getting distracted from the Phase 1 thinking and activities, you may experience the connection with your Higher Self without doing anything else (so you won't even need Chapter 4). Good news, right?

The reason behind this is that being connected with your Higher Self is your natural state. The Phase 1 game is just a distraction.

Hugs

Although hugs could be categorized under 'movement' or 'distraction', they receive a special mention.

Why?

Because they can do many things at once: the simple act of hugging is such an incredible way to not only bond with others but to also boost your physical and emotional health.

The scientific reason is that when you hug someone for at least 20 seconds, the neuropeptide oxytocin is produced. It is a naturally occurring hormone in your body with incredibly powerful, health-giving properties. It's our naturally occurring mood enhancer.

A 10-20 second hug a day can lead to biochemical and physiological reactions in your body that can significantly improve your health.

This includes:
- Lower risk of heart disease
- Stress reduction
- Fight fatigue
- Boost your immune system
- Fight infections
- Ease depression

Now, many people are not used to hugging, or for personal reasons, they just prefer not to be hugged. The reason is that when the wicked warriors are in defense mode, they want to keep all possible attacks at a distance, both literally and figuratively. As a consequence most human touch is avoided.

Dealing with hugs can be a challenge, especially when you feel that there is no balance in the exchange. For example, the other person doesn't want to 'share a hug', but is 'demanding' one. Or when the other person is deeply immersed in the Phase 1 game (and may be radiating 'negative' energy).

What I want to invite you to do, is to really go for the experience of the benefits of hugs in a safe way.

This is how you can approach this:

- Feel first where the other person is. Preferably they are in their center. However, if they are still in Phase 1 mode, but not playing it out, this may already be enough.
- If you can be, and stay, in your own center, that would be ideal. However, when you are overwhelmed, this probably won't be the case.
- Say to yourself, "I accept the comforting and compassion. Every other need I leave with the other person."
- When you are not in a situation where you are overwhelmed, consider a hug as an opportunity to exchange good vibes. If you want to, you can say to yourself, "I happily accept the good vibes from you. I'm glad I can give you good vibes as well. Every other need you may have I leave with you. Every other need I may have I leave with myself."

I hope to have shown you that it is less difficult to get out of a 'negative' emotion or an overwhelming feeling than most people think. Don't underestimate the simplicity of the methods I just shared!

More background information about breathing, voice work, flower remedies, movement, distraction and hugging can be found in the Library on the website.

Techniques and Tools

Once you have found some stress relief from a big panic attack, or when you are aware of what is happening during the attack, you may want to look for what has caused that panic attack or strong emotional reaction.

I call it *looking at your monsters*.

Once you have identified a monster and have honestly looked at it, you can transform it. You can take its power away, reclaim it for yourself and then look at what the monster really is: simply a teddy bear who was all the time by your side to support and comfort you.

In this sub chapter you will find a few of the many techniques or tools that can help you with releasing stress. Hopefully this chapter will help you understand what is going on and show you how to turn a situation around.

EFT or Emotional Freedom Techniques (Gary Craig)

EFT, or Emotional Freedom Techniques, is also known as the 'tapping technique', because you will be using your fingers to tap on several meridians in your body.

I will share with you the Basic Tapping Procedure from Gary Craig. It is called 'basic' because it is the foundation for tapping. You can add other techniques later if you choose. However, this basic procedure will be enough in most cases.

The explanation that follows comes from Gary's website (**www.emofree.com**).

The Basic Tapping Procedure — The Centerpiece of EFT

The EFT Tapping Basic Recipe is an easy to use healing tool that provides the very foundation for expanding your emotional freedom.

The EFT Tapping Basic Recipe has only five brief steps (ingredients) and takes very little effort to learn. Once memorized, each round of tapping can be performed in about 30 seconds. It will take some practice of course, but after a few tries the whole process becomes familiar enough that you can do it in your sleep (millions have done this technique, including children and the elderly). Once you learn this technique you will then have a permanent tool that you can use for a lifetime.

The EFT Tapping Points

These illustrations, together with the written aids below them, are self-explanatory. For now, just locate each of these points on your own body and touch each of them with your fingertips.

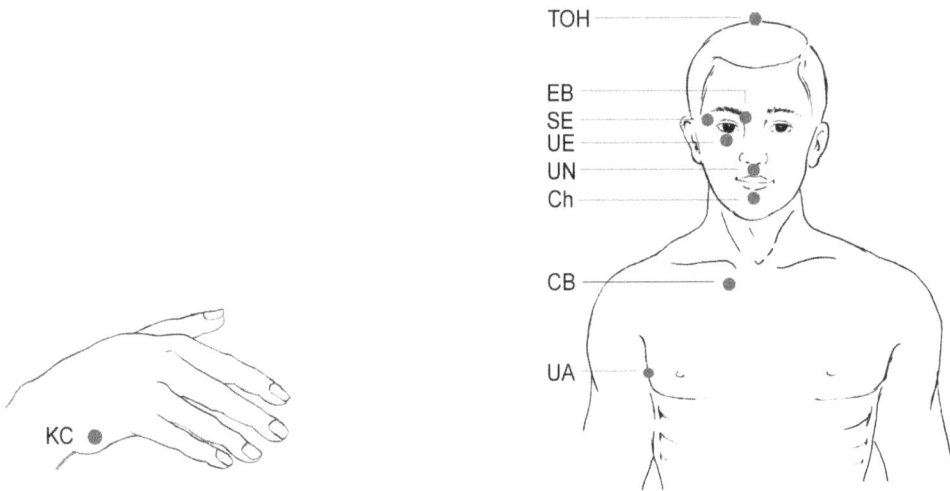

KC: The Karate Chop point (abbreviated KC) is located at the center of the fleshy part of the outside of your hand (either hand) between the top of the wrist and the base of the baby finger. For those of you familiar with martial arts, it's the part of your hand you would use to deliver a karate chop.

TOH: On the top of the head. If you were to draw a line from one ear, over the head, to the other ear, and another line from your nose to the back of your neck, the TOH point is where those two lines would intersect.

EB: At the beginning of the eyebrow, just above and to one side of the nose. This point is abbreviated EB for beginning of the Eye Brow.

SE: On the bone bordering the outside corner of the eye. This point is abbreviated SE for Side of the Eye.

UE: On the bone under an eye about 1-inch below your pupil. This point is abbreviated UE for Under the Eye.

UN: On the small area between the bottom of your nose and the top of your upper lip. This point is abbreviated UN for Under the Nose.

Ch: Midway between the point of your chin and the bottom of your lower lip. Even though it is not directly on the point of the chin, we call it the chin point because it is descriptive enough for people to understand easily. This point is abbreviated Ch for Chin.

CB: The junction where the sternum (breastbone), collarbone and the first rib meet. To locate it, first place your forefinger on the U-shaped notch at the top of the breastbone (about where a man would knot his tie). From the bottom of the U, move your forefinger down toward the navel 1 inch and then go to the left (or right) 1 inch. This point is abbreviated CB for CollarBone even though it is not on the collarbone (or clavicle) per se. It is at the beginning of the collarbone and we call it the collarbone point because that is a lot easier to say than, 'the junction where the sternum (breastbone), collarbone and the first rib meet'.

UA: On the side of the body, at a point even with the nipple (for men) or in the middle of the bra strap (for women). It is about 4 inches below the armpit. This point is abbreviated UA for Under the Arm.

Tapping Tips

These tips answer the most common questions beginners have about tapping.

Some of the Tapping points have twin points on each side of the body. For example, the 'eyebrow' point on the right side of the body has a twin point on the left side of the body. Years of experience have taught us that you only need to tap one of these twin points. However, if you have both hands free you can certainly tap on both sides for good measure.

You can also switch sides when you tap these points. For example, during the same round of The EFT Tapping Basic Recipe, you can tap the 'karate chop' point on your left hand and the eyebrow point on the right side of your body. This makes the Tapping process more convenient to perform.

The Tapping is done with two or more fingertips. This is so you can cover a larger area and thereby insure that your Tapping covers the correct point. While you can tap with the fingertips of either hand, most people use their dominant hand. For example, right handed people tap with the fingertips of their right hand while left handed people tap with the fingertips of their left hand.

You tap approximately five times on each point. No need to count the taps because anywhere between three and seven taps on each point is adequate. The only exception is during the Setup step (explained later) where the Karate Chop Point is tapped continuously while you repeat some standard wording.

The process is easily memorized. After you have tapped the Karate Chop Point, the rest of the points go down the body (see the Sequence Points in the diagram above). The Eyebrow point, for example, is below the Top of the Head point. The Side of the Eye point is below the Eyebrow point. And so on down the body.

The 5 Steps of The EFT Tapping Basic Recipe

1. Identify the Issue:

All you do here is make a mental note of what ails you. This becomes the target at which you 'aim' the EFT Tapping Basic Recipe. Examples may be: Sore shoulder, my father embarrassing me at my 8-year-old birthday party, or not being able to hit that high singing note and sounding like I was squawking rather than singing. You may have a lot of issues, but be sure you are only targeting one issue at a time. Trying to combine issues in the process will compromise your results.

2. Test the Initial Intensity:

Here you establish a before level of the issue's intensity. Do this by assigning a number to the issue on a 0-10 scale where 10 is the worst the issue has ever been and 0 is no problem whatsoever. This serves as a benchmark so we can compare our progress after each round of The EFT Tapping Basic Recipe. If, for example, we start at an eight and eventually reach a four, then we know we have achieved a 50% improvement. The number of possible issues we can address with The EFT Tapping Basic Recipe is endless. The issues don't all fit into neat testing boxes. That is why there is an entire segment on dedicated to 'Testing Your EFT Tapping Work' on Gary Craig's website. For this stage of your learning, however, here are some useful methods to help you access your issue(s) and arrive at your 0-10 numbers. They apply to most issues.

- For emotional issues, you can recreate the memories in your mind and assess their discomforts.
- For physical ailments you can simply assess the existing pain or discomfort.
- For performance issues you can attempt the desired performance level and measure how close you come to it.

3. The Setup:

The Setup is a process we use to start each round of Tapping. By designing a simple phrase and saying it while continuously tapping the KC point, you let your system know what you're trying to address.

When designing this phrase there are two goals to achieve:

1) Acknowledge the problem
2) Accept yourself in spite of it

We do this by saying:

"Even though I have this _____, I deeply and completely accept myself."

The blank above represents the problem you want to address, so you can just insert things like:

This sore shoulder:

"Even though I have this sore shoulder, I deeply and completely accept myself."

This fear of spiders:

"Even though I have this fear of spiders, I deeply and completely accept myself."

This humiliation at my eighth grade graduation:

"Even though I have this humiliation at my eighth grade graduation, I deeply and completely accept myself."

This difficulty making free throws:

"Even though I have this difficulty making free throws, I deeply and completely accept myself."

Not all of the issues will fit neatly into "Even though I have this _____." Don't worry, you can use some flexibility when designing your Setup phrase. For example, instead of ',this sore shoulder' you could say "Even though my shoulder hurts, I deeply and completely accept myself." Or instead of, "this humiliation at my eighth grade graduation" you could say, "Even though my dad humiliated me at my eighth grade graduation."

By using "Even though I have this _____," you will automatically choose something that represents your experience, your reaction, or a problem that you recognize as something that belongs to you, and that is an important feature.

We do not want to use EFT on someone else's problem. For example, rather than, "Even though my son is addicted to drugs, I deeply and completely accept myself," it's better to focus on your own reaction, which may be, "Even though I'm frustrated by my son's drug addiction." Or instead of "Even though my husband works too much," it's better to try something like, "Even though I feel alone when my husband stays late at the office…" We want to aim EFT at *our* part of the problem rather than trying to fix someone else's problem.

By identifying the problem with this phrase, you 'set up' the initial zzzzzt (energy disruption) behind the scenes so the tapping has something to resolve.

Important, Important, Important:

The language that we use always aims at the negative. This is essential because it is the negative that creates the energy disruptions (zzzzzts) that the EFT Tapping Basic Recipe clears (and thus brings peace to the system). By contrast, conventional methods and popular self-help books stress positive thinking and preach avoiding the negative. This sounds good but, for our purposes it does little more than cover over the negative with pleasant sounding words. EFT, on the other hand, needs to aim at the negative so it can be neutralized. This allows our natural positives to bubble up to the top.

4. The Sequence:

This is the workhorse part of The EFT Tapping Basic Recipe that stimulates/balances the body's energy pathways. To perform it, you tap each of the points shown in the Sequence Points diagram (see above) while saying a Reminder Phrase that keeps your system tuned into the issue. I list the points below followed by a description of the Reminder Phrase:

1. Top of the Head (TOH)
2. Beginning of the Eyebrow (EB)
3. Side of the Eye (SE)
4. Under the Eye (UE)
5. Under the Nose (UN)
6. Chin Point (CH)
7. Beginning of the Collarbone (CB)
8. Under the Arm (UA)

The Reminder Phrase is quite simple as you need only identify the issue with some brief wording. Depending on your issue, you may say the following at each tapping point....

"This sore shoulder,"
"My father embarrassed me,"
"This difficulty in singing that high note."

5. Test the Intensity Again:

Finally, you establish an 'after' level of the issue's intensity by assigning a number to it on a 0-10 scale. You compare this with the before level to see how much progress you have made. If you are not down to zero then repeat the process until you either achieve zero or plateau at some level.

Extra tips about EFT can be found in the Library on the website.

Focus Wheel Process (Esther and Jerry Hicks, Teachings of Abraham)

I learned this exercise in the book *Ask and It is Given* (by Esther and Jerry Hicks, **www.abraham-hicks.com**). It is a process that is found in lot of their work. I heard examples on CDs and videos and read about it in some other books by them as well.

Let's first look at an explanation of the exercise, and then at an example.

Draw a large circle on a sheet of paper. Then draw a smaller circle, about two inches in diameter, in the center of the large circle. Sit back and look at the small circle and feel your eyes focus upon it.

Now, close your eyes for a moment and turn your attention to whatever has happened that has produced the negative emotion within you. Identify what it is that you do not want.

At this point, say to yourself: "Well, I clearly know what I don't want. What is it that I do want?" It is helpful if you try to identify what you do not want as well as what you do want in terms of the way you want to feel about it.

For example,

- I feel fat, and I want to feel slender.
- I feel poor, and I want to feel prosperous.
- I feel unloved, and I want to feel loved.
- I feel deceived, and I want to feel honored.
- I feel ill, and I want to feel well.
- I feel powerless, and I want to feel my power.

Next, try to write statements around the outside edge of your large circle that match what it is that you *do* want. When you find a statement that is a close enough match, you will know it. In other words, you will *feel* whether your statement does not match and throws you off the wheel and into the bushes, so to speak. Or you'll know whether it is a statement that is close enough to your desire that it sticks.

The reason the Focus Wheel Process is so effective is because the statements you are writing are those that you have deliberately chosen. They are general statements that you already believe, that match your desire(s).

As you find thoughts that feel good, continue writing them around the perimeter of your larger circle. Start at what 12 o'clock would be if you were looking at a clock, and then continue around to 1 o'clock, 2 o'clock, and so on, until you have 12 statements that feel good to you.

Sometimes your thoughts are already spinning with such momentum that even though you want to change them you cannot find a place to jump in. This Focus Wheel game is about finding a thought that is close enough to where you are right now so that you do not end up being thrown off. Instead, you can gradually begin moving toward the way you want to feel. It is a wonderful vibrational bridging tool. (Or to use the words from this book: a wonderful tool to get from the outpost into your center).

Example:

Let's say that you feel fat. Something has happened in your experience to bring that to the forefront of your mind and you are, in this moment, feeling strong negative emotions about it. Take your paper, draw a circle in the center of the page, and within the circle you could write the words: I want to feel slender.

Now, focus upon the subject at hand and try to find thoughts that match how you want to feel, thoughts that feel good to you while you ponder them. Try to find a thought that does not throw you off in the bushes.

"I can be slender again."

This thought is too far from what you really believe, and while you want to believe it, you do not. You can actually feel that you do not quite yet feel this way. And so, because this thought does not *feel* good to you, this is an off-in-the-bushes statement.

"My sisters are slender and beautiful."

This thought does not feel good either. It points out their success and makes you feel your own lack of success even more. This thought throws you off in the bushes.

"I'll find something that will work for me."

While this thought feels a little bit better than the previous ones, it still does not feel good. You have tried many things, including diet and exercising, but you believe that you have found nothing that works for you like you want, so this thought just points out your past failures. This thought throws you off in the bushes.

"I know that there are others who have been where I now am who have found a way that works for them."

With this thought, you may feel a sensation of relief. You do feel a little bit better. Remember, you are not looking for the end-all solution here. You are only looking for a thought that feels good enough that it sticks. And this thought does not throw you off in the bushes. So, write it on your page at the 12 o'clock position, and now you reach for more good-feeling thoughts.

"I don't have to do all of this today." (That is another one that sticks. Write it at the 1 o'clock position.)

"I'll find a diet that works." (Off in the bushes.)

"I don't feel good in my clothes." (Off in the bushes.)

"It will be fun to buy some new clothes." (2:00) (That one sticks.)

"My body will feel more refreshed." (3:00) (That one sticks.)

"I will feel more vital." (4:00) (Sticks.)

"New ideas will come to me." (5:00) (You're rolling now)

"I already know some things that will help." (6:00) (Yes, feeling better)

"I like taking control of my own experience." (7:00) (Sticks.)

"I'm looking forward to making this change." (8:00) (Sticks.)

"I like feeling good." (9:00) (That one sticks.)

"I like feeling good in my body." (10:00) (Sticks.)

"I feel good about my body." (11:00)

Yes! Now, after writing on the 11:00 position, empathically circle the words you originally wrote in the center of your Focus Wheel, and notice that you now do feel a closer vibrational alignment with that thought, when only minutes before, you were nowhere near that vibration.

You can do this Focus Wheel Process not only when you feel bad, but also when you feel neutral or good so you can feel even better. Or in other words: you can use it no matter what game you are playing: the Phase 1 game or Phase 2 or 3 game.

Note: if you want to do this Focus Wheel Process, set aside 15 to 20 minutes to complete it.

The Work (Byron Katie)

This process was developed by Byron Katie. Byron Katie is the author of a.o. *Loving What Is, Who Would You Be Without Your Story* and *I Need Your Love — Is That True?* Her website is: **www.thework.com**.

The main concept behind Katie's work is that we are responsible for everything in our lives, that what we perceive in others shows us the way to our own fears, our own monsters and helps us to release the power that people, thoughts or situations have over us.

When to use it? For me it is a method that is primarily useful when you are **triggered by a person**.

This is the worksheet '**Judge Your Neighbor**' *(© 2014 Byron Katie International, Inc. All rights reserved. thework.com)* that you'll need to do the Work.

Basically it comes down to 3 steps:

1. Judge your neighbor and write it down
2. Ask four questions
3. Turn it around

Step 1: Judge your neighbor and write it down

Fill in the blanks below, writing about someone (dead or alive) you haven't yet forgiven one hundred percent. Use short, simple sentences. Don't censor yourself—try to fully experience the anger or pain as if the situation were occurring right now. Take this opportunity to express your judgments on paper.

1. In this situation, time, and location, who angers, confuses, or disappoints you, and why? (For example, I am angry with Paul because he doesn't listen to me about his health.)

   I am _____ (emotion) with _____ (name) because
   _____

2. In this situation, how do you want them to change? What do you want them to do? (For example, I want Paul to see that he is wrong. I want him to stop lying to me. I want him to see that he is killing himself.)

   I want _____ (name) to _____
   _____

106

3. In this situation, what advice would you offer to them? (For example, Paul should take a deep breath. He should calm down. He should see that his behavior frightens me. He should know that being right is not worth another heart attack.)

    _____ (name) should/shouldn't _____
    _____

4. In order for **you** to be happy in this situation, what do you need them to think, say, feel, or do? (For example, I need Paul to hear me when I talk to him. I need him to take care of himself. I need him to admit that I am right.)

    I need _____ (name) to _____
    _____

5. What do you think of them in this situation? Make a list. (For example, Paul is unfair, arrogant, loud, dishonest, way out of line, and unconscious.)

    _____ (name) is _____
    _____

6. What is it in or about this situation that you don't ever want to experience again? (For example, I don't ever want Paul to lie to me again. I don't ever want to see him ruining his health again.).

    I don't ever want _____
    _____

Do you really want to look at what is going on? Investigate each of your statements using the four questions and the turnaround below. The Work is about creating more awareness. Ask the questions, then go inside and wait for the deeper answers to surface.

Step 2: The Four questions

For example, Paul doesn't listen to me about his health.

1. **Is it true? Yes or no.** (If no, go to question 3).
2. **Can you absolutely know that it's true?** Yes or no. If yes: can you really know everything about a person? Everything about his background or history?
3. **How do you react when you think that thought?** What kind of feelings do you experience? Anger, sadness, frustration? Does it bring stress or peace?
4. **Who would you be without the thought?** Close your eyes. Picture yourself in the presence of the person you are thinking of. Now imagine looking at that person, just for a moment, without the thought. What do you see? What would your life look like without that thought?

Step 3: The Turnaround

Next, turn your statement around. The turnarounds are an opportunity to consider the opposite of what you believe to be true. You may find several turnarounds.

Turn the thought around:

a) to the self. (For example, I don't listen to myself about my health.)
b) to the other. (For example, I don't listen to Paul about his health.)
c) to the opposite. (For example, Paul does listen to me about his health.)

Then find at least three specific, genuine examples of how each turnaround is true for you in this situation.

Now do the same for statement two to six. For statement six there is a special instruction: replace the words "I don't ever want to ..." with "I am willing to ..." and "I look forward to ..." This is about welcoming all your thoughts and experiences with open arms. In many cases this is enough to transform your fear, your monster into a teddy bear.

Until you can look forward to all aspects of life without fear, your Work is not done. But be gentle with yourself. It is not a competition or a race ☺. And you still have plenty of time to discover many more monsters and turn them into teddy bears.

Core Quadrants (Daniel Ofman)

In Chapters 1 and 2 we already saw that there are gifts to be found in the interaction with people, and also in situations we experience more as 'negative'.

An excellent model to use these more 'negative' experiences with is the Core Quadrant model of Daniel Ofman. He is the author of *Fancy meeting me here* and many other books explaining how core quadrants work. There is also the Iphone/Android App "Core Quality". Much more information regarding core quadrants can be found on **www.corequality.nl**.

The Quadrant model allows us to discover the gifts these negative experiences contain.

This is what the Core Quadrant (or Core Qualities) model looks like:

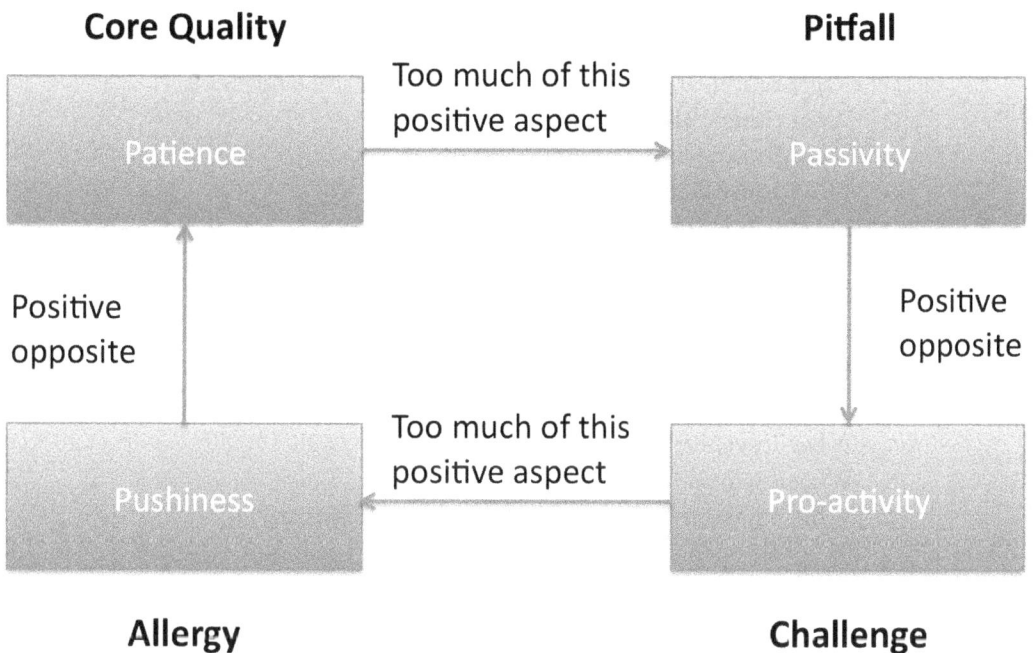

Core Quality		Pitfall
Patience	Too much of this positive aspect →	Passivity
↑ Positive opposite		Positive opposite ↓
Pushiness	← Too much of this positive aspect	Pro-activity
Allergy		Challenge

How does it work?

Let's use an example, starting top left and rotating clockwise.

- The Core Quality this person has is Patience.
- Too much of this Core Quality (which is a positive quality) is Passivity. This is the Pitfall for this person.
- The positive opposite of the Pitfall is Pro-activity. This is this person's Challenge.
- Too much of this Challenge (which is a positive quality) is Pushiness. That is this person's Allergy.
- The positive opposite of the Allergy is Patience. And we are back at the Core Quality.

Here is a list with some more details to provide you with a better understanding of what the quadrants entail.

- Core quality: positive quality
  - What I think is normal (about me)
  - What others appreciate about me
  - What I encourage in others
  - What I expect from others or demand
- Pitfall: exaggeration of a positive quality so it becomes negative
  - What others blame me for
  - What I am willing to forgive in others
  - What I justify about myself
- Challenge: positive quality, opposite of core quality, that is asking to be balanced in our life
  - What I admire in others
  - What I lack in myself
  - What others wish for me
- Allergy: exaggeration of a positive quality so it becomes negative
  - What I despise in others
  - What I would hate in myself
  - What I have to tolerate in others (but hardly can)

What does it mean in practice?

Core quality: this is a strength, something that comes natural to you, but not to others. They think it is amazing that you have this talent. But most of the times you think it is no big deal, just because it comes naturally. Many times there is a blind spot here. At the same time many people feel that they are not worth that much or don't have much to contribute. So the goal is to see and acknowledge your qualities again.

Pitfall: this is too much of a core quality. This is what people blame you for. This is one of the ways they attack you from their Phase 1 state. The consequence is that since we feel attacked on the pitfall, we don't look at the core quality either.

Challenge: this is something that you wanted to experience more in this lifetime. Sometimes it is something to balance your life with (to feel less stress, to become neutral again). Sometimes it is something that gives you more joy. However most of the times we don't see it because the path to it is blocked.

Allergy: this is the 'negative' opposite of a core quality. This is what pushes your buttons. This is one way we use to attack other people within our Phase 1 game.

The core quadrants model helps on the one hand to discover both your Core Quality and Challenge and on the other hand to be less judging towards other people because you will understand from which core quality or challenge their behavior originates.

The interesting thing about this model is that you can start using it from every angle. Since we mostly act from our Phase 1 mechanism, the most obvious angles to start with are:

- Allergy: your blames or complaints about other people
- Pitfall: other people's blames or complaints about you

Starting from the allergy or pitfall we can easily discover our core talents and challenges. First this will be reducing stress because you know more what your core qualities are on the one hand and what it is that you may want to balance out more on the other hand. Secondly it helps to discover where you may find more joy.

It also helps in your interactions with other people.

Every time you hear yourself judge someone (blaming or complaining because you are 'allergic' to their behavior), stop yourself and wonder: which positive quality is this too much of? To which challenge is this person pointing me? The answer you receive is a quality you can play with more yourself. It is a quality that can help you become more balanced, more centered. Or you can ask yourself: what is the positive opposite of this behavior that I'm allergic to? To which core quality is this person pointing me?

Also, every time someone judges you (they blame you, or complain about you), instead of getting defensive right away, consider it as an invitation to look at one of your core qualities that you just put too much energy in. When you hear someone blame you, think about which positive quality there is too much of. In this way you can discover a core quality, something you are really good at. Or they may point you to a challenge: the positive opposite of the blame.

Since many times our core qualities are blind spots to us and the challenges are unknown, this model of core qualities may offer great insights very quickly by starting from a pitfall or allergy.

Besides getting more insights, you may get a totally different perspective on this person who is blaming you or to whom you are allergic: instead of pushing him away, you can thank him for his contribution (you can just do this in your mind, you don't have to speak it out). And what happens many times afterwards: they change their behavior or disappear from your life. In other words: once you have accepted their gift, they move on to something else.

You can even go beyond this: you can also use the model to relax your judgment about others, see them more in a neutral light or even discover their lovable core qualities! The simple way to do this is to start from your allergy and then think about which quality this is too much of. Then you see their core quality (which is your challenge).

You can take it a step further and create a double core quadrant. You can then discover how your allergy may be their pitfall. That then is the reason why you clash so much. At the same time you can discover their core quality, your own core quality and your challenge.

If you are interested in knowing more about double core quadrants, please visit the Library on the website.

Extra dimension

When working with the model, I have discovered that an extra dimension can be added. Besides the existing 'guardians' towards the challenge (pitfall and allergy) a third one can be added: fear. Or to keep the analogy of the book in mind: monsters.

When a fear comes up, when a monster rears its ugly head, it is not always possible to translate that into the core quadrants model. On the other hand, it is also showing the way to a core quality and a challenge. Now, most of the time it is related to an allergy, but at the same time it is hard to translate it into one. Especially when we are sort of paralyzed by the monster.

Remember the example I gave about my relationships with women? That I was retracting love and then creating a break in the relationship when I felt that I did not have enough time for myself? Let's use that situation as an example.

The extra dimension to the model includes looking at both the behavior and the underlying fear.

This is what it looks like:

- Behavior: retracting love or attention from a loved one.
- Underlying fear: there is (or will be) not enough time for myself.
- Challenge (positive opposite): having enough time for myself.
- Allergy: egoistic behavior.
- Core Quality: supporting others.
- Pitfall: rescuing others.

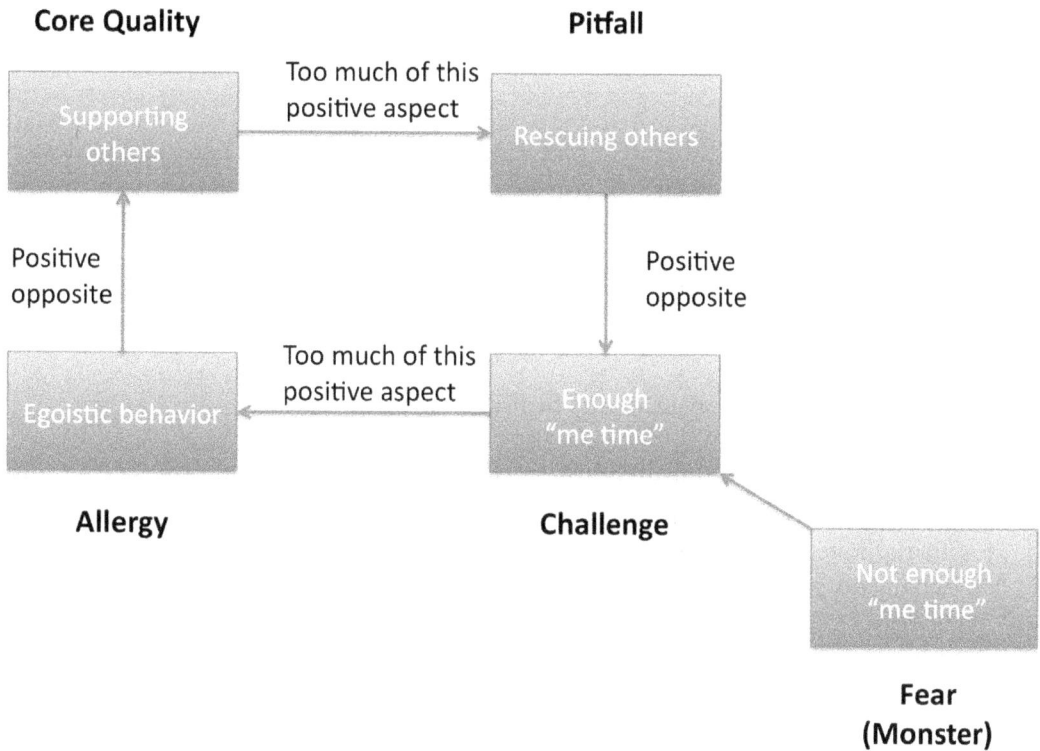

Going from a fear-based game to a love-based one

Using core quadrants is one way to assist you in playing the Phase 2 and 3 game instead of the Phase 1 game.

Let's take a closer look at our last example:

- Behavior: retracting love or attention from a loved one.
- Underlying fear: there is, or will not be, enough time for myself.
- Challenge (positive opposite): having enough time for myself.
- Allergy: egoistic behavior.
- Core Quality: supporting others.
- Pitfall: rescuing others.

In the Phase 1 game, your wicked warriors would be focused on the fear and looking for situations and people that demand your time. Because you don't want people demanding your time, you feel attacked and you will retaliate.

In the love-based game, your merry minstrels would be focused on the challenge and looking for situations and people that support you in having plenty of 'me time'. That could translate into less people that need you, people that leave you alone or people who live their life fairly independently and who don't look to you for help. It could also be situations where an appointment is cancelled, a customer quits or even a disease that forces you to rest. These things all give you more 'me time'. Now the last examples may seem 'negative'. However, if you look from a love-based perspective, they are not.

What will happen if you deliberately play the love-based game? There will be less of those 'negative' situations. Why? If you are playing the Phase 1 game, you are not paying attention to all the options you have for having more 'me time'. And then your Higher Self has to come up with more 'convincing' ways (like an illness or accident) to do it. When you are playing the love-based game, you will see the options much faster. As a consequence they will be much lighter!

When we go back to the monster-teddy bear analogy:

- In the fear-based game of Phase 1, the monster is blocking the way to what you want, to what makes you happy and joyful, to what gives you energy.
- In the love-based game of Phase 2 and 3, the teddy bear is inviting you to do what you want, to do what makes you happy and joyful, to what gives you energy.

More background information, exercises, video clips, and extra tips about EFT, The Focus Wheel, The Work, Core Quadrants and their 'inventors' can be found in the Library on the website. You can also find coaches, therapists and healers who work with these methods in the free Directory.

Turning monsters into teddy bears

As I mentioned a few times in the book, I encountered some fears in the period before and during writing it.

They were scary fears! Fortunately I have learned that they are just monsters that are trying to keep me away from 'the treasures'. I also know that I'm playing the Phase 1 game when these fears show up as monsters. So when they showed up, I took a deep breath (yes, time and again, because they didn't show up all at once ☺) and I reminded myself that they are simply, 'wrongly washed teddy bears' that are showing me where I can find my power.

Secondly, what was even scarier was worrying about others learning about my fears. And again I realized that there was a treasure there as well. I realized that it was just another monster, on another level. Sharing my fears would defeat the monster and turn it into a teddy bear.

Then I thought, as I'm already sharing my fears with you, why not use them as examples to show how I dealt with them to explain how the model of transforming monsters into teddy bears works?

So here they are.

I proudly present: Jan's fears! ☺

Fear 1: I'm also just a student of how this all works. Who am I to write a book about this topic? I need to be an expert who has read, digested, and lived all there is to know about this before I can even do a small attempt to share a small piece of it.

These are the steps I used to deal with this fear:

- I was willing to look at the monster that was trying to keep me small. I was willing to observe it, not to fight it or to run away from it.
- Then I became aware that I was identifying with what an author should look like and that these identifications were monsters trying to keep me away from my talents.
- I used EFT to remove the energy block so I was calm again. Then I allowed myself to have another picture of what an author should be. I changed the identification. I changed my limiting beliefs. As a result the monster was a lot smaller and wasn't so scary anymore.
- I was honest to myself about the fear. In this way it didn't remain a hidden power/tool for the wicked warriors to use. I could embrace the monster with compassion.
- I was willing to be vulnerable. The best way to do this was to share my fears with lots of people. The book was ideal for that purpose ☺.
- I realized that the monster was a 'wrongly washed teddy bear'. I realized that I put it there to enjoy the Human Game. When I perceived it as a monster, I felt powerless. I gave my power away to the monster. But after going through the previous steps I could see it as a cute teddy bear that gives me energy. The teddy bear shows me the way to my unlimited power source from which I can write, speak and live!

Fear 2: Will my corporate clients (who know me from the topics 'business networking' and 'LinkedIn') accept me presenting this topic? Won't it be too airy-fairy for them? Won't they reject me (although the foundation in my previous books also was of spiritual nature)?

These are the steps I used to deal with this fear:

- I was willing to look at the monster from all angles.
- Since it was quite overwhelming I used the flower essence Terra to calm me down.
- Once I was less upset I became aware that I was still looking to other people for approval. I also realized I was afraid of a lack of money.
- I made a list of all the people I was still seeking approval of. I used Ho'oponopono to ask them, and also myself, for forgiveness. I also used Ho'oponopono to ask my Higher Self to forgive me for not always trusting that It would take care of me financially by having people buy the book, or that

people would hire me for presentations or other ways I couldn't think of myself.

- I was honest with myself about these fears. In this way it didn't remain a hidden power/tool for the wicked warriors to use. It also gave me a feeling of liberation.
- I was willing to be vulnerable by sharing these fears in the book.
- I saw that the monster was a wrongly washed teddy bear. I could now see that the teddy bear was showing me the way to the cave with my talents and abundance.

Next fears:
- **Will readers from my previous work appreciate the book?**
  - **Will they buy it?**
  - **Will they reject me or laugh at me because of the content?**
- **Will I have enough money to publish the book?**
- **Will I have enough money to survive while taking this whole new path in my life?**

These three fears came at the same time. And yes, they were quite overwhelming ☺. These are the steps I used to deal with them:

- I was willing to look at the monsters. I was willing to not fight them or run away from them, but to observe them.
- As I did this I became aware that there were still deeper levels of fear, including the fear of lack and the fear of rejection.
- To get out of the 'negative' feeling that pushed me into the Phase 1 game, I used EFT. When I was calmer, I recalled all the lovely comments about the previous books. Some were heart warming, others revealed how life changing the books had been. I also realized that selling a book is just one of the ways money can flow in. I made a list of other ways (presentations, workshops, training courses, webinars, donations, coaching, book deals, e-courses ...). These were all ways that I had used in the past. The first thing that happened is that I realized once again how many ways there are for good things to manifest. What happens when someone (me in this case) is in the Phase 1 game, is that they get stuck with one option and don't see the rest anymore? They limit themselves. The second thing that happened in the days after I looked at the monsters was that the idea of crowdfunding came into my mind. I also noticed an email (that I normally just would have deleted straight away) about the win-win loan. This is a loan that someone in Flanders gives to a small business. They get tax benefits for doing that. In other words, once I had realized my options and get out of the Phase 1 energy, my Higher Self added two very interesting options to the list.
- I was honest to myself about the monsters. In this way they didn't remain a hidden power/tool for the wicked warriors to use.

- I was willing to be vulnerable by sharing them in the book.
- I realized that by being willing to look at the monsters, I could liberate myself from limiting beliefs. As I experienced that the monsters suddenly changed into teddy bears I noticed solutions I'd never thought of.

Then the next batch:
1. **The book has to be perfect. It has to be complete. It has to be logical. There can't be any paragraph in the book that may give anyone reason for criticism (attack).**
2. **Can I use smileys in the book? That won't be perceived as professional.**
3. **When I add the list with fears in the book, won't people laugh with them and perceive me as weak?**

These three fears came also more or less at the same time (over a period of one-to-two days). This is how I dealt with them:

- I was willing to look at the monsters.
- Then I became aware that they were monsters regarding rejection (again!) and how many different faces this one fear has.
- Since I had been working on the fear of rejection for a while (including the fears I shared above), these monsters weren't so big. I was able to go to my center very quickly by using the focus method (visualizing a small ball dropping in from above the head into the heart region, see chapter 4). Once I was in my center I could start lovingly challenging the fears:
  - **Does it have to be perfect?** "It can't be. There is always something else to add and always other metaphors and analogies that might appeal more to one person than to another."
  - **Does it have to be complete?** "A book can't be complete. There is a limited number of pages. One way to deal with this is to add extra information on the website **www.life-is-a-game.org**. There I can also add video and audio. So that is a good way to deal with this fear. Creating a series of books that go deeper into other topics like relationships, money, and the body also feels liberating. In that way the book can remain around 200 pages instead of 500. That will make things much easier."
  - **It has to be logical. There can't be any paragraph in the book that may give reason for criticism (attack).** "Wow, that is a Phase 1 game way of thinking ☺. Life isn't only logical. That was a nice try of the wicked warriors to stay in control. Let's thank them again for their excellent service during Phase 1 of my game. And give them another assignment: be on the lookout for ways to spot love and to extend love."
  - **Can I use smileys in the book? That won't be perceived as professional.** "My intention with this book is to share how light life

can be. Laughter is an essential part of that. Smileys are a current way of expression that is written in both online and offline communication. So they absolutely belong in the book." By connecting with my intention, the fear disappeared almost instantly!

- **When I add the list with fears in the book, won't people laugh with them and perceive me as weak?** "I have the experience of how liberating it is to be honest, open and transparent. I also felt how empowering it is to be vulnerable. When being vulnerable there is no attack from my side and there is nothing to be attacked by anybody else. By being vulnerable I become invulnerable." However I realized that this had sometimes been a mental explanation by the wicked warriors. But since I immediately felt the power in me, I realized it was not the wicked warriors, but my Higher Self that had whispered in my ear to be vulnerable.

- I was honest to myself about this. In this way it didn't remain a hidden power/tool for the wicked warriors to use.
- I was willing to be vulnerable by sharing the fears in the book.
- The monsters were transformed into teddy bears that are not only a power source. They are also supporting me and cheering me on in living a joyful life!

So you see: just like any other human being I have fears. I have played the Phase 1 game, and still play it now and again.

But since I'm committed to living in a more centered way, and to be totally honest with what's happening, I'm more quickly aware when I'm playing the Phase 1 game.

To sum up, let's look at the general approach I use to transform monsters into teddy bears.

This is the model for transforming monsters into teddy bears, which I also call the 'transformation model':

1. I'm willing to look at the monster. Willingness and deliberately choosing to transform fears is a crucial first step. And the best thing is that it only takes less than a second to do this!

2. If it is really overwhelming I use a flower essence like Terra or Rescue to calm me down a bit.

3. I'm committed to look at all angles of the monster, or at all the monsters that are standing behind the first one. Most of the time I realize that there are just a bunch of little monsters standing on each other's shoulders pretending to be a very big and very scary monster.

4. I use one of the Emergency Tools or Techniques (if necessary). Sometimes I can quickly see what is going on without having to use any tools or techniques. The result could be less stress, more insights, practical solutions,…

5. I'm honest with myself about the fears and the monsters. In this way they don't remain a hidden power/tool for the wicked warriors to use. The monsters have become smaller over time and can now be embraced with compassion.

6. I'm willing to be vulnerable and to show/share my monsters. Again willingness is the catalyst for transformation. I know from experience that by being vulnerable I become invulnerable.

7. I see the monsters as 'wrongly washed teddy bears'. They are not only a power source, but they are also supporting me and cheering me on in living a joyful life!

Other tools, techniques and support

I already mentioned flower remedies being such a big help for an immediate release of stress or when you are overwhelmed by your emotions.

What I also have discovered from my personal experience is that there are many other things that can help us as well.

I will list a few of them. Because a detailed explanation is beyond the scope of this book, I refer to the Library on the website for more information.

Crystals

Just like human bodies (and everything else), crystals and gemstones have a vibrational frequency as well.

A typical characteristic of crystals is that they can have a strong influence on the energy of their environment. This means they have a positive influence on the energy of an individual person when the person is wearing gemstone jewels or carrying a small crystal in their pocket. Secondly larger crystals or gemstones also have an influence on an entire room. And they are also very pretty to look at ☺. This alone can help reduce stress.

From my personal experience they have beneficial effects when placed in a living room (to create more harmony for example), in a bed room (for better sleep), or in a room where therapists, coaches or healers work (to support the processes of the clients).

Feng Shui

Crystals are also often part of Feng Shui.

Feng Shui is the science and art of how to create an environment that is harmonious for the people who live or work in it.

For me Feng Shui is a blend of creating a living or working space that looks good (visual and rational) and feels good (invisible and energetic).

I experienced that I was more relaxed after applying these tips, which allowed me to float more easily from my outpost to my center.

Heart coherence

Another way of immediately reducing overwhelming feelings is to pay attention to your heart coherence.

On the website you will find a compact explanation of what heart coherence is about. It is from the Heartmath website, the institution that is specialized in this subject.

The Process (Robert Scheinfeld)

The Process is a technique I learned from Robert Scheinfeld (**www.robertscheinfeld.com**). You can find it in his book *Busting Loose from the Money Game*. That book was one of the clues on my road, together with *Busting Loose from the Business Game*. Both books and the process itself, are very much related to what I'm sharing with you in this book. If you feel inspired, also read one or both of Scheinfeld's books!

The Process is a technique for facing your fears (your monsters) and regaining the power you gave away to them.

When to use it? For me it is a method that is very useful when you feel stressed about a situation. It's for when you feel your stomach contracting because of a 'negative' emotion, or when you feel 'bad' in any way because of something that is happening or has (just) happened to you.

In my opinion it is also a method that is primarily useful when you are **triggered by a situation.** The 'Judge Your Neighbour' exercise from Byron Katie's *The Work* is more suited when you are **triggered by a person.**

Systemic work or Constellations

Although it is hard to explain systemic work (or constellations) to someone who has never experienced a session, I will give it a try ☺.

In general: just as DNA is passed from generation to generation to generation, energetic patterns are also passed on. In other words, we don't only inherit specific body characteristics, but also energetic ones.

I have received lots of benefits from systemic work. I got both more insights in where the blocks were as (immediate) changes in my daily life. I also witnessed many 'miraculous' changes in other peoples' lives as well.

So why don't you look at the directory of coaches, therapists, healers and facilitators on the website to find someone near you who organizes sessions?

Note: please remember that the 'methods' from this chapter are still tools to use. They are not the goal or final solution. I see many people look at them as their ultimate salvation (which is sometimes another form of the victim-rescuer game, not with people, but with tools or techniques). For me the benefit of these tools and techniques is that they can help you get away from being distracted by pain or fear. When you're not distracted you can give your attention solely to moving from your outpost to your center. When you are in your center, you can focus on consciously connecting with your Higher Self.

For more background information about Heart Coherence, Systemic Work, The Process, Feng Shui and Crystals, and who can help you find the right gems and stones for you, see the Library on the website ***www.life-is-a-game.org***. *If you live in Belgium, a great shop for beautiful crystals and for Feng Shui materials is 'Het Vliegend Konijn'* ***(www.hetvliegendkonijn.be)***.

Not me, but my friend needs urgent help. What can I do?

There will be a great many times in your life where you don't need support, but a friend, partner, child or relative does.

For me those times have been the moments that I have felt I was both the most powerless man in the world, yet also the most powerful one. I didn't feel these things at the same time, although there were incidents where I went from feeling totally powerless to very powerful. These moments happen to all of us. We all experience moments where we can assist someone, or hopelessly fail to do so. These can be among the most intense moments in your life.

So let's look what **you can** do when a friend can use some support.

Step 1: Be very honest about your own role.

Are you there as someone who can be a neutral and objective supporter? Or is there a victim-rescuer game at play? Be very honest about it, because the clues may be very subtle. You never do your friend or yourself, a favor by playing the victim-rescuer game.

Sometimes it may be hard to realize that you have been in such a game, but when you honestly admit it to yourself, miracles can start to happen. If you are able to recognize what's happening, you have probably been practicing several ways to relax the wicked warriors. So it won't really come as a shock to you. Then what will happen? After a potential whiff of guilt, you suddenly will be thrown into your center. You even can tell your friend that you just realized that you were playing the victim-rescuer game. And if you can do that from your centered position instead of from the outpost, that may be all that's needed for your friend to relax and float towards his or her own center.

Now, let's assume you were not in the victim-rescuer game (or were not aware of it). The key of the first step is to move out of your own outpost and into your center before doing anything else. If you are in Phase 1 mode and reacting from it, you won't be of much real help to your friend. Actually, if you are in your outpost, it may be better to remove yourself (temporarily) from the situation. In that way, you won't be (sub)consciously feeding the fears or the stressful situation. You may say: "I will go outside for a few minutes. But be reassured, I'm still here and I will come back. I'm here to support you."

Step 2: Help them to calm down a bit.

The easiest thing to do is to remind them to breathe deeply.

Step 3: Be with them from your center.

From your center (whether or not you're consciously connected to your Higher Self), focus on them. What works very well for me, is to say the four sentences of the Ho'oponopono inside my own mind and heart with a focus on them.

What I have experienced is that it keeps me in my center and most of the time it calms them as well. They even start to float towards their center, without anything else being done!

Step 4: Use a technique

Sometimes the first three steps are enough. Your friend will feel they got genuine attention (not pitiful attention), which empowers them to take their power back. Or at least find enough power to take the next step by themselves.

If they are asking for more information or help, or if you feel something else can be done, you can invite them to do one of the processes I described in this chapter, along with you. Which process? That depends. Maybe it's one that they know and feel comfortable with. Maybe it's one that you have used yourself and feel confident doing with them. Maybe the both of you feel that the best option is to try out a new one.

Follow your gut feeling or intuition. Even if you are afraid to do so, remember that it doesn't have to be perfect. In case you get stuck, try something else. Just keep your intention in mind: you want to be there for your friend, from your center. Everything that happens is OK and is what needs to happen at this moment in time.

Even if you didn't get anywhere trying one of the techniques, you still did step one, two and three. Your friend should be feeling already a lot better and more capable of taking certain actions or making certain decisions. If (s)he feels that a certain technique may help, (s)he may contact a professional that can help him or her with it.

Directory of coaches, therapists, healers and facilitators

In this chapter you've found several ways to release stress and to transform your monsters into teddy bears. I hope it is clear that in principle you don't need anyone else.

However, sometimes there are situations where one could use some support and more professional help. That is why there is a directory of coaches, therapists, facilitators and healers on the website **www.life-is-a-game.org**. Not only are they more neutral (and not feeding your fear-based thoughts nor playing the victim-rescuer game), but they also are more skilled in several techniques and tools and have more experience in using them.

So if you need any help with one or more of the techniques or models or just are open for any technique and want to find someone neutral to your situation in your neighborhood, consult the website.

Notes:
- Coaches, therapists, healers and facilitators can put their contact details on the website for free. The reason that this service is provided is that I want to have anyone in the world to have access to at least some other person who can support him or her.
- I haven't screened them so always follow your gut feeling about whether or not to work with someone. If it helps you to make a better decision, look at their website, LinkedIn page or Facebook page first or ask for an intake/interview or references.
- People are adding their contact details daily, so please go back on a regular basis to see if there is someone new in your area with a particular specialty.

Chapter 4: Getting into alignment with your Higher Self

In the two previous chapters we learned how to relax your wicked warriors and get out of the outpost. As a result of getting out of that place of stress you'll see you'll begin to float towards your center. Now let's continue the movement towards the center and get more consciously connected. In the previous chapters our goal was about moving *away* from the outpost. In this chapter our goal is about moving more deliberately *towards* the center. Once you can do that, then you can consciously connect with your Higher Self.

The good news is that there are many ways to get consciously connected with your Higher Self, to get aligned with it. You're not limited to one path, one technique or one tool. Since everybody's path in life is different, not surprisingly we all have our preferences about how to connect or align with our Higher Self. Whatever approach you decide upon, the first step is to **make the conscious choice** to get away from the outpost and move towards your center.

In Chapter 2 there are several 'Invitations' to loosen up the wicked warriors. The more you have consciously applied and practiced those Invitations, the more you are already in your center, and the easier it is to consciously feel the connection with your Higher Self. As you applied some of the methods or techniques from Chapter 3, you also moved towards your center. You may have already experienced being consciously connected.

In this chapter the main idea is becoming aligned first with your Higher Self before taking any action. First BE-ing before DO-ing. We live in a three-dimensional world, which is an action-oriented dimension. Therefore our lives exist from and because of our actions. In other words, it is not about *only* BE-ing, but about first BE-ing in order to take inspired action afterwards. Simply put: DO-ing inspired by BE-ing. This will ensure we live a much lighter and more effortless life. In other words: more en-light-enment. That being said, there are many ways to become aligned. Because being connected to your Higher Self is your natural state, just relaxing the wicked warriors may get you aligned without doing anything else.

In this chapter I will share a few rather simple and fun ways to become more consciously connected with your Higher Self. Feel for yourself what works for you. I have deliberately kept the explanation as short as possible so you can see how simple it is. If you want to know more about a specific way, there are more examples and background info in the *Library* on the website.

Way 1: Use your feelings as your guiding mechanism

The most quoted source I have found for using your feelings as a guiding mechanism are the *Teachings of Abraham*, by Esther and Jerry Hicks (www.abraham-hicks.com). They can be found in several books of which *Ask And It Is Given* is the best-known one.

My short version of *The Teachings of Abraham* regarding this topic is:
- Your Higher Self holds the overview and is always on the lookout for the best life possible, based upon what you want and what you don't want.
- Your feelings are your guiding mechanism to see whether or not you are in alignment with your Higher Self (and the best life possible).
- When it feels 'positive', you are more aligned with your Higher Self.
- When it feels 'negative', you are less aligned with your Higher Self and are more in resistance.

This is the scale with 22 emotions (from the book *Ask and It is Given*), the Emotional Guidance Scale:

1. Joy/Knowledge/Empowerment/Freedom/Love/Appreciation
2. Passion
3. Enthusiasm/Eagerness/Happiness
4. Positive Expectation/Belief
5. Optimism
6. Hopefulness
7. Contentment
8. Boredom
9. Pessimism
10. Frustration/Irritation/Impatience
11. "Overwhelment"
12. Disappointment
13. Doubt
14. Worry
15. Blame
16. Discouragement
17. Anger
18. Revenge
19. Hatred/Rage
20. Jealousy
21. Insecurity/Guilt/Unworthiness
22. Fear/Grief/Depression/Despair/Powerlessness

Downstream

Upstream

One of the analogies the Hicks use is that of a canoe on the river. The river has a directional stream. You can go along with it (downstream) or go against it (upstream). When you go upstream, you will feel resistance and any paddling you do will take more energy than needed. The river is an analogy for life. Life happens anyway. You can choose to follow the current of life or go against it. Your Higher Self will let you know what you are doing: when you are more in the lower numbers (1-7) of the emotional scale, you are letting the current carry you. When you are in the higher numbers (8-22) you are going upstream, resisting the current of life.

I would like to add my own shortened version of this approach: when something feels 'light' you are more in alignment with your Higher Self. When something feels 'heavy' you are less aligned. For me it is sometimes easier to use this approach than the 22 emotions scale. And it avoids the *positive vs. negative* connotation that many people struggle with.

Many detailed insights regarding certain situations in life and exercises can be found in the Hicks' books *The Amazing Power of Deliberate Intent, The Astonishing Power of Emotions, Money, and the Law of Attraction,* and several others (see www.abraham-hicks.com).

One of the exercises from *Ask and It is Given* is the Focus Wheel Process that we already used in Chapter 3. This is an exercise or process designed to take us from a more *negative* emotion to a less *negative* or more *positive* emotion. It is about finding relief. This is an excellent example for when you are still in your outpost (but are aware of it) or already in your center, but still feeling heavy.

Another exercise for when you are already centered and feeling good and wanting to strengthen the connection with your Higher Self is the *Rampage of Appreciation Game*.

Let's use the description from *Ask and It Is Given* to explain how it works.

The *Rampage of Appreciation Game* can be played anywhere and at any time. It is a game that is easily played simply by directing pleasant thoughts in your mind. If you were to write your thoughts on paper, it would enhance this process, but it is not necessary.

Begin by looking around your immediate environment and noticing something that pleases you. Try to hold your attention on this pleasing object as you consider how wonderful, beautiful, or useful it is. And as you focus upon it longer, your positive feelings about it will increase.

Now, notice your improved feeling, and appreciate the way you're feeling. Once your good feeling is noticeably stronger than when you began, look around your environment and choose another pleasing object for your positive attention.

Make it your objective to choose objects of attention that easily evoke your appreciation. This is not a process of finding something troubling and fixing it. It's a process of observation and appreciation. The longer you focus upon things that feel good to you, the easier it is for you to maintain those vibrational frequencies that feel good. And the more you maintain those good-feeling frequencies, the more other thoughts, experiences, people, and things that match your practiced vibration will appear in your life.

Since it is your primary intention to find things to appreciate, you are practicing a vibration of less resistance, and you are making your connection to your Higher Self stronger. Because the vibration of appreciation is the most powerful connection between your Human Form and your Higher Self, this process will also put you in a position to receive even clearer guidance from your Higher Self. The more you find something to appreciate, the better it feels; the better it feels, the more you want to do it; the more you do it, the better it feels; the better it feels … the more you want to do it.

When you are playing this game, keep playing for as long as you have the time and for as long as it feels good. If you attempt this game and you do not feel good, or if the practice annoys you for any reason, then stop playing. If the momentum isn't picking up after a few attempts, then choose another game like the Focus Wheel process.

At first, it would be a good idea to deliberately set aside 10 or 15 minutes a day to specifically practice this process. After a few days of enjoying the benefit of deliberately achieving and maintaining a raised vibration, you will find yourself doing it many times during every day. Even if you just practice a few seconds here and a few seconds there, in a variety of situations, you'll enjoy it just because it feels so pleasing.

For example, while standing in line at the post office, you may think:

> This is a very nice building.
> It's great that they keep it so clean.
> I like how friendly that postal worker is.
> I appreciate the way that that mother is interacting with her child.
> That's a good-looking jacket.
> My day is really going well.

You could focus more specifically on any of your objects of appreciation and find even more reasons to feel appreciation. For example,

- This is a very nice building …
- There is so much more parking space here than at the old post office.
- There are more counters here, and the lines move much faster than before.
- The big windows make this room feel much airier.

130

Once you become more oriented toward looking for things to appreciate, you will find that your day will be filled with such observations. Your thoughts and feelings of appreciation will flow from you naturally. And often, while in the midst of a genuine feeling of appreciation for someone or something, you will feel ripples of goose bumps — those sensations are confirming your alignment with your Higher Self.

Every time you appreciate something, every time you praise something, every time you feel good about something, you are telling your Higher Self: "More of this, please." You need never make another verbal statement of this intent, and if you are mostly in a state of appreciation, all good things will flow to you.

A desire to appreciate things and people around you is a very good first step. As you find more things that you would like to say "Thank you" about, your process will quickly gain momentum. If you want to feel appreciation, you attract something to appreciate. And as you appreciate it, then you attract something else to appreciate, until, in time, you are experiencing a *Rampage of Appreciation*.

Way 2: Meditation

Meditation has been around for thousands of years. You will find references to it in all personal and spiritual growth and religious books, teachings and traditions.

However, I have always had a resistance to practicing it. So I took a deeper look and discovered a few misperceptions that I had.

The first step was actually not a misperception, but the realization that my wicked warriors were heavily resisting my curiosity about meditation. Let alone my practicing it. Recognizing what was going on there was a first important step.

Then I looked at my thoughts and beliefs about meditation: "You have to sit in silence for hours and no thought is allowed to pass by."

Now that is a heavy rule, especially when you are just starting a new practice ☺.

Although for some people sitting in silence for hours with no thoughts passing by is the way to go, there are other elements to take into consideration.

1. No activity

In the physical world, life is about taking action. Sitting still with your head in the clouds because it feels so good is not what you came here to do in this physical body (but if you feel good doing it, who am I to judge ☺). It is a privilege to be here on Earth, to be able to feel, touch, smell; to use our senses and our body. I think my Higher Self is very jealous of that, because in its non-physical form It can't have that experience. For me life is about inspired action. Action inspired by my connection with my Higher Self. This is not about taking action because I need or have to do something because my wicked warriors fear that otherwise I won't survive (or will be attacked). It is about inspired action.

2. Time

You don't have to meditate for hours. The aim is to get connected and be inspired so you can go about your day in a 'light' energy in which everything happens effortlessly (or when 'heavy' things happen, you can deal with them rather easily). This can go very quickly, especially when you consciously connect with your Higher Self more often.

3. Silence

You can also meditate without being in silence. Being caught up in an activity that you enjoy is also a kind of meditation. When you are 'in flow', with an activity that is also meditation. For example, Gwendolyn told me that she is in meditation mode when she is cooking.

4. No thoughts

Why do most spiritual traditions say to have *no thoughts* when meditating? Because it is most of the time easier to go from *negative* thoughts to no thoughts than directly to *positive, connected* thoughts.

It is like riding with a train in one direction at high speed. It needs to slow down first, then stop, reverse and then accelerate before it can go at high speed in the other direction. If it would be mechanically possible to do otherwise and go from full speed in one direction to full speed in the other one, it would be extremely uncomfortable for the passengers. And they would most likely resist taking the train in the future.

So with meditation and other methods we use to connect to our Higher Self it is kind of the same story. If a method or practice would horribly shake you, your wicked warriors might say, "This is a bad experience, we need to protect you/us from this attack again. So whenever meditation comes up, we will make you run as far as fast as you can."

The idea behind meditation is in the first place not to be distracted by Phase 1 thoughts. Not being distracted will free up space for inspiration from your Higher Self. So you still may get thoughts and ideas during your meditation, but instead of feeling *heavy*, they feel *light*, pleasurable and give you joy.

For example,
- *Heavy* thoughts may be about things like: tax paying, cleaning or other chores, something that *needs* to be done (but that you don't like doing), etc.
- *Light* thoughts may be about things like: a solution to a problem, an extra insight to be included in an article or book, warm feelings in your body, a loving thought about someone or something, etc.

Personally, it works for me like this: from the moment I feel I can't wait to do something because I'm so excited by it, the meditation can end. If I do the meditation by myself I can always come back to it after writing down the inspired idea, but most of the time I know that period of meditation has been enough. In other words: I invite you to not make meditation a ritual that needs to be done in a specific way for a specific amount of time. Just follow the flow.

5. ... no thought is allowed to pass by ...

When I hear that I can't do something, my wicked warriors rise up in resistance immediately. So I have learned to translate those words to an invitation instead: "You are invited to have no thoughts." In this way there is less, or no resistance, in giving it a try.

How to meditate?

There are several ways to meditate.

A simple approach is to just get into silence. Find a quiet place and relax your mind.

However, since most people are not used to connecting with silence to begin with, there are other approaches you can try.

Let's use the description of a meditation exercise from the book, *Ask and It Is Given.*

> Sit in a quiet space where you are not likely to be interrupted. Wear comfortable clothing. It does not matter if you sit in a chair or on the floor, or even lie in your bed (unless you tend to fall asleep when doing so). The important thing is that your body is comfortable.
>
> Now, close your eyes, relax and breathe. Slowly draw air into your lungs, and then enjoy the comfortable release of that air. Your personal comfort here is very important.
>
> As your mind begins to wander, gently release any thought(s) you may have; or at least do not encourage them by pondering them further. Refocus upon your breathing.
>
> Because you are by nature a human being, you'll want to focus on something. So in the beginning meditation will feel unnatural. You will find your mind wanting to return to things you have previously focused on. When that happens, relax, breathe again, and try to release the thought.
>
> You will find it easier to quiet your mind if you will choose small thoughts that do not have the potential for expanding into something interesting. You could focus upon your own breathing. You could mentally count your breaths, as they go in and out. You could listen to the dripping of a faucet. In choosing whatever soft, gentle thought you chose, you will leave behind the thoughts of resistance. As a consequence your state of vibration will rise to its natural, pure state.

It helps to set your intention to thinking about nothing more than being in this moment, and in being consciously aware of your breathing.

As you quiet your mind, you may feel a sense of physical detachment. For example, you may feel no real difference between your toe and your nose. Sometimes you will feel a sensation of twitching and itching beneath your skin. And often, once you have released resistance and are soaring in your natural pure, high vibrations, you will feel an involuntary movement in your body. It may sway slightly from side to side or forward and backward, or your head may roll gently from side to side. Or, you may simply feel a general sensation of movement or of a yawn. Any or all of these sensations or movements are indicators of your achievement of a state of meditation.

Do this for 10 to 15 minutes every day and your life will change. You will be more centered and much more easily consciously connected with your Higher Self.

If you like sound or have a hard time focusing on your breathing, you could use a mantra.

Why are mantras used?

I found this explanation from Deepak Chopra very useful.

Silently repeating a mantra as you meditate is a powerful way to enter the silence of the mind. As you repeat the mantra, it creates a mental vibration that allows the mind to experience deeper levels of awareness. As you meditate, the mantra becomes increasingly abstract and indistinct, until you're finally led into the field of pure consciousness from which the vibration arose.

Repetition of the mantra helps you disconnect from the thoughts filling your mind so that perhaps you may slip into the gap between thoughts. The mantra is a tool to support your meditation practice. Mantras can be viewed as ancient power words with subtle intentions that help us connect to spirit, the source of everything in the universe. As you experience deeper meditative states, all thoughts and worries drop away and you experience the quiet that always exists beneath the noisy internal dialogue of the mind. In this stillness you may feel oneness with all life and profound peace.

Most of the times words from the Vedic tradition are used, but you can also use an affirmation instead (see below).

Examples of mantras:

- Om Dakini Namaha (English: I activate my security)
- Om Rakini Namaha (English: I activate my happiness)
- Om Lakini Namaha (English: I activate my power)
- Om Kakini Namaha (English: I activate my love)
- Om Shakini Namaha (English: I activate my creativity)
- Om Hakini Namaha (English: I activate my intuition)
- Om Katyayani Namaha (English: I activate my pure awareness)

The idea is to use one mantra (or one affirmation) per day. You repeat this one sentence over and over again. You can say it out loud by yourself or with other people.

Sometimes it is easier to be guided in a meditation or in singing or reciting mantras. There are many good CDs and MP3s out there to choose from.

Way 3: Prayer

To be honest, I was resistant to the word 'prayer' because it reminded me too much of my Catholic upbringing. Now, don't get me wrong; I didn't go to church a lot, but apparently a Catholic school and a Jesuit college (and a family with Catholic influences as well) still planted somehow some seeds in me, however subtle they were.

Although I haven't done a full search of what kind of seeds they are, a few of them definitely showed up at several times in my life:

- Guilt
- Shame
- "You NEED to be good (to go to Heaven)"

Besides that, praying had a connotation for me of people who felt like a victim and were hoping to be miraculously saved by God (or an angel or a saint).

I always felt resistance to people who relied on others instead of taking action for themselves.

However, now I understand that:

- Do-ing (action) is only necessary after Be-ing inspired
- Not all prayers are about asking to be saved
- Not all prayers are asked from a victim perspective

Praying can also include:

- Talking to your Higher Self (or God, angels, saints, Spirit, the Universe) without needing something
- Expressing gratitude
- Asking for guidance, help, inspiration from a centered position (not from the outpost or from the victim position)

In practice praying can come in many forms.

You can just talk like you are having a conversation. Or you can create your own words and lines and then say, sing or write them.

You can use existing prayers, lyrics from songs or other texts. If you do this, please make sure you feel the words. Choose the ones that move you, not because they are popular or are used in your spiritual group. Maybe you are even the only one who likes a specific prayer. It doesn't matter as long as it appeals to you.

Of course you can do whatever you want ☺. The reason I'm putting so much emphasis on it, is that when you feel nothing with specific lyrics and you are using them anyway, chances are high your wicked warriors are at play: "I MUST do this, otherwise I'm not a good spiritual person." Or they may be playing the game of blending in so you won't be rejected.

A prayer can be short, it can be long, and it can also be a song. One that I like a lot is the song *Thank you* from Amitabhan. You can listen to it (and even download it) on his website: **http://www.amitabhan.com/pages/music.html**

Way 4: Affirmations

You've probably already heard about affirmations.

When this term is used in personal and spiritual growth environments, it's describing the short and positive sentences you say, out loud, about yourself. What most people don't realize is that they are already using affirmations all the time! Every time you say: "I am …" you are affirming something.

For example,
* "I am stupid."
* "I am smart."
* "I am clumsy."
* "I am cool."
* "I am not OK."
* "I am a horrible cook."
* "I am an excellent driver."

Positive or negative, they are all affirmations.

Now the interesting thing is how the wicked warriors and your Higher Self react to them.

The wicked warriors believe the *negative* affirmations (they value them as *true*) and doubt the *positive* ones (they value them as *false* or at best they think they are neutral). This may seem contrary to what we have seen before about the wicked warriors defending the thoughts we have valued as true, but it isn't.

For example, you have the belief that you are an excellent driver. When someone else says anything that could imply something else, the wicked warriors will defend your belief. At the same time, when you are in the outpost, there is always an underlying thought that you're not worthy enough. Self-doubt is always present. In other words: while the wicked warriors defend the *positive* belief to the outside world, inside they are questioning and doubting you and themselves.

On the other hand, Your Higher Self is always happy when you say positive things about yourself. It doesn't believe the negative affirmations because Your Higher Self sees from Its helicopter perspective that those negative affirmations are not true anyway. At the same time your Higher Self is assisting you in playing the game on Earth. So, no matter what experience you are asking for, *negative* or *positive*, you'll get it. So whenever you say a negative affirmation, like "I'm a horrible cook", your Higher Self will create circumstances that seem to validate that belief.

For example, your children may complain about your cooking. You can then choose to believe the negative affirmation again, or you can decide to choose something else. For example you can stop saying anything at all about your skills in the kitchen. Or you may say something like, "I am learning to cook good meals. Every time I cook I learn new ways about what works and what doesn't. I am happy with my experience."

The more you are aware of the power of "I AM" statements and the more you start using them in a way to positively affirm yourself, the more joyous experiences you'll have.

Here are some examples of affirmations you can use.

These are some to start with:
- I am good.
- I am a loving person.
- I am healthy.
- I am smart.
- I am perfect the way I am.

You could use one of the affirmations Robert Scheinfeld uses for *The Process*:
- "I am the Power and Presence of God."
- "I am the Power of Infinite Intelligence."
- "I am the Power of Pure Consciousness."
- "I am the Ultimate Power in the Universe."

These are a few other ones:
- I AM an Unlimited Being playing the human game.
- I AM pure Love.
- I AM pure Light.

Actually, the words "I AM" are enough.

"I AM" means:
- "I": it is about your whole Being, both physical and non-physical.
- "AM": … is present, here and now.
- "I AM": I'm present, here and now, as a whole Being.

However, if you are just starting your journey, this may be too hard for your mind to grasp.

Anyway, it is always important to use affirmations that feel good and right to you. Don't use someone else's affirmations because you fear that you won't do the right thing if you create your own. Just play with them!

Way 5: Turn the wicked warriors into merry minstrels

In Chapter 1 I explained that the wicked warriors are small robots that automatically perform the task they were given—helping us to survive. They are the brilliant helpers needed to play the Phase 1 game.

Now that we understand that the world is a neutral place and have stepped into Phase 2, it's not necessary for our wicked warriors to be on a constant look out for danger anymore. However, they are still powerful assistants, so it would be a waste to let them become unemployed. So let's give them a different role. Let's reprogram them. Let's turn them into merry minstrels.

Instead of permanently being on the lookout for danger, let's invite them to be on a constant look out for expressions of love, such as people, objects and experiences to be grateful for.

Our fear-based wicked warriors become the love-based merry minstrels if we reprogram them. They will still live in the outpost because they still need to function like an antenna. However they are no longer looking out for danger. And when you visit the outpost, they will no longer try to convince you that there is danger everywhere. Once we reprogram them, they will no longer collect evidence of the war-like behavior of others.

They would be looking for people who have also chosen to live their lives from their center. Or, they will look for people who could use an infusion of love. They're no longer looking for people to save, but people to support in a healthy way. That support may be a smile, a hug, or just to being present with someone from your center in order to inspire them to leave their outpost. They will no longer try to convince you of anything, but they will show you how neutral and harmless the world actually is. They no longer collect evidence of anything, but continue to show you what wonderful creations are possible on the game board of planet Earth.

In this way you are also less likely to automatically go back to Phase 1. The more wicked warriors have been turned into merry minstrels, the less loud their call is when they perceive danger. As a consequence you won't be overwhelmed by them. And it will be easier to stay in your center.

How can you reprogram them? Actually, it is rather easy.

When you perceive an attack, remind yourself: "This is coming to my attention to be healed in one way or the other."

Every time you are able to look at what is happening and stay out of Phase 1 a wicked warrior becomes a neutral robot. When you are able to turn the situation around and interact from love, the neutral robot is turned into a merry minstrel. That's how easy it is.

However, in the beginning it may appear nothing is happening. It's like losing a great deal of weight. When you want to lose 100 pounds, the visual loss of the first 10 pounds is almost invisible because there is still much left. It's the same with the wicked warriors.

Let's assume that you have 100 wicked warriors. When you have turned one of them into a neutral robot or a merry minstrel then there are still 99 screaming wicked warriors left. It's hard to notice the loss of one voice. So they will continue to make a lot of noise. However, after some time that will change when there are less wicked warriors and more merry minstrels. Then you will feel less stress and much more love and appreciation for life!

Way 6: Soul Body Fusion®

While most spiritual traditions encourage meditating in order to make contact with their Higher Self, Jonette Crowley has a different approach with her Soul Body Fusion (**www.soulbodyfusion.com**).

What happens with many people who meditate deeply? They are consciously connected with their Higher Self in the 'higher realms' and many times feel sad when they 'return in their body'.

The Soul Body Fusion approach is to work the other way around: instead of going up to your Higher Self in the non-physical realm, the fusion approach is about inviting your Higher Self to come down to meet in the physical realm, in your body.

The good news is that it is a very easy process that you can do with a partner or alone.

This is the description of how to do it alone from the book, *Soul Body Fusion*.

There are 4 steps in the process:
1. Set your intention
2. Sit with your feet on the floor and with the palms of your hands up
3. Be present, stay in your body, don't go into the higher realms
4. Observe your experience, don't judge, analyze or compare and don't try to fix anything

Step 1: Set your intention

Say out loud or in your mind that it is your intention to harmonize the frequencies of your body with those of your Higher Self. You want your cells to adapt to permanently hold more of your own light, energy, and divineness. Don't worry about the exact words you use. The energy of your intention is what matters.

Step 2: Sit with your feet on the floor and with the palms of your hands up

The reason to put your feet on the floor is to help you ground yourself. If you prefer lying on the floor, that is also OK. There are no exact rules in Soul Body Fusion! The reason for holding the palms of your hands up is that people often feel energy, warmth, tingles in the palms of their hands. Holding them up makes this experience easier.

Step 3: Be present, stay in your body, don't go into the 'higher realms'

This is important since the goal is to integrate your higher dimensions in your body and your daily life, not to continue the separation between spirit and matter. Often it can be a habit to leave the body and meet your Higher Self in the higher realms. That is not the goal! Stay grounded, present and anchored in your body.

Step 4: Observe your experience, don't judge, analyze or compare and don't try to fix anything

The easiest way to stay focused is to keep yourself busy with observing of what happens during the process. Do your hands get warm? Do you feel tingles? What happens with your legs and feet? What happens with your arms? What else is changing? What do you feel, physically and emotionally? The emphasis is on feeling so you don't start thinking too much.

Just observe what happens and keep an open mind for whatever insights and experiences you may get. Don't try to understand why this happens and don't try to change it, stimulate it or fix it. Trust the process. Your experience is exactly what it needs to be. Every feeling, comfortable or not, is perfect. If you don't feel anything at all—perfect. No judgment. The most difficult part of this simple process is to *do* nothing.

What does a Soul Body Fusion session look like?

Set aside 25 minutes for this exercise. You can have a pen and paper ready to write down your experiences afterwards. Also have a glass of water ready. Drinking water will help to integrate the influx of energy.

Phase 1: 10 minutes

Do the 4 steps of the process. Keep observing what happens. This will keep your mind from wandering away. Ten minutes is usually enough time to feel changes and sensations.

Take a break

After 10 minutes you can take a short break (5 minutes). You may write down what you have experienced, or not. Drink some water.

Phase 2: 10 minutes

Do the 4 steps again. Due to the energetic break this next phase may bring in a different experience. Even if you have only 5 minutes per phase, it is better to do two phases with a break than 10 minutes straight.

Ending the Soul Body Fusion

Drink another glass of water and write down your impressions. It helps to just note your experiences, not your thoughts about them. Listen to your intuition. Is it necessary to add a third phase? Do you need fresh air? Do you need to move? Do you feel like dancing? Some people have the feeling they just had some kind of surgery and need to sleep. Other people have so much energy that they start cleaning the house. Most of the time you want to spend some time alone to integrate. Ask yourself: "What is the best thing for me to do right now?" Follow your intuition.

For a video from Jonette Crowley where she guides you through the process, visit the Library on the website. In her book there is also a description of how to do a Soul Body Fusion session with someone else.

Way 7: Focus

The previous exercises have described different approaches and practices to get more aligned with your Higher Self.

What happened in all of them was you:

- Made a conscious decision to align with your Higher Self
- Used a method to focus

Focus is critical, so it's important you find a way to focus that works for you. One method I learned in the Touch of Matrix course is to get your personality out of the way. *(Note: Touch of Matrix is a healing method that is related to Reiki, Quantum Touch and Reconnective Healing if you'd like to explore it more.).*

This process of getting your personality (or wicked warriors) out of the way and becoming aligned with your Higher Self before you actually give a healing session to the client is important for achieving the results the client wants. The good news is that you can always apply this method, whether or not you are giving healing sessions to someone.

How do you do that?

Simply envision a small ball dropping in from the top of your head (crown chakra) to your heart region (heart chakra).

Even if it doesn't work to find alignment with your Higher Self right away, it will help you to become easily centered. At least that is my experience ☺.

*More information about the topics of this chapter can be found in the Library on the website **www.life-is-a-game.org**, including :*
- *A selection of mantras and guided meditations and extra information about meditation.*
- *More background information about affirmations and "I AM" affirmations.*
- *A video where Jonette Crowley shows how Soul Body Fusion works.*
- *A short description of healing methods like Touch of Matrix, Reiki, Quantum Touch and Reconnective Healing.*

Chapter 5: Creating a Joyous Human Life — Attracting What You Want

In the previous chapters, the focus was on moving from the outpost towards the center. Once you're at your center then you begin to be more consciously connected to your Higher Self. As a result you already feel much lighter and experience more joy, happiness and effortlessness.

In this chapter we will look at how you can attract more situations, people and things in your life that you enjoy. By attracting those things and people you will feel even better. It's actually not really necessary to have, do or be more to feel great (like we will see in Chapter 6), but since we are living as Human Forms in an experience based environment, we do enjoy the interactions with the world.

So let's see how we can attract what we want.

You probably have already heard of the 'Law of Attraction'. Apparently, the term was introduced in *The Teachings of Abraham* (Esther and Jerry Hicks). Later on it was adopted by many other teachers and authors and popularized in the movie, *The Secret*.

The Law of Attraction is a concept I have been using in my life for a while now. For example, it helped to turn my books *Let's Connect!* and *How to REALLY use LinkedIn* into international best sellers. And at the same time I felt that I was missing some pieces of the puzzle because the results were not consistent and I didn't feel fulfilled.

Inconsistent results brought me to a deeper examination of the different aspects of the Law of Attraction as I searched for the missing pieces. I will share those with you in this part of the book. In the meantime, I also found out that the reason I didn't feel fulfilled was that I was not aware of the game I was playing. I was still playing the Phase 1 game instead of the Joyful Game of Life.

When you are still in the Phase 1 game, no results will really satisfy you. Whatever you get, whatever you achieve, you still will feel that there is something missing. Finding satisfaction can be another thing to strive for. But when you have achieved that, after a period of satisfaction, something starts nagging again. In Phase 1 of the human game you can never be never satisfied. And besides that, the more material possessions you collect, the more stuff the wicked warriors feel they need to protect. The more stuff you have, the more there is to be worried about, and the more stress is generated as your warriors need to watch over everything to make sure it is not attacked, damaged or stolen.

It is only when we are consciously connected to our Higher Self that we can feel the peace we are so frantically looking for in Phase 1 of the human game. We then start doing less and being more, with peace and quiet as a result. And at the same time, when we are connected, we will be doing more than ever before. Because when our Do-ing is inspired by our Be-ing, nothing feels heavy anymore. Everything flows smoothly and effortlessly. We are carried and guided by our Higher Selves so the total experience feels different.

This may result (or not) in material wealth. But with no attachment to that wealth if we gain it. It is the attachment to things and the thoughts around them that creates the battles in Phase 1. When we release the attachments, we naturally float towards our center.

When you are consciously connected with your Higher Self you also know that you will be taken care of. So even if you lose all material stuff at one moment, you know that you will be OK. You know that in one way or the other it will come back. If it doesn't return, maybe you were consciously or subconsciously longing for a life of simplicity. What I'm saying is, either way it doesn't matter anymore.

If you are reading these words and you are at this moment in your outpost with your wicked warriors, you may not believe a word I'm writing here. That's OK. Or maybe you want to believe the words, but you feel a huge struggle inside of you (the wicked warriors are demanding attention). For me this was a big insight: applying 'center-based' tips from any spiritual tradition while being in the outpost doesn't provide results (or at least not any consistent ones). As a consequence I thought I was doing something wrong, that I was not good enough. I'm so glad now that I understand the dynamics behind what happened and I hope you feel the same way after reading this book!

So if you don't believe a word I'm writing or if you feel a giant battle going on inside of you, then this part of the book is not for you yet. But if you start paying attention to the tips I shared in the previous chapters of the book, you will definitely be ready for it one day (and probably much sooner than later). And even if I don't know you personally, I really wish for you that you would experience it in this lifetime!

However the good news is that even if you are still spending much more time in your outpost instead of in your center, and even if you are still immersed quite deeply in Phase 1, and even if your aren't feeling the peace yet, the 'Law of Attraction' may help you to see the changes you desire in your daily life.

So let's look at what the Law of Attraction really entails.

The Law of Attraction

We know from quantum physics that everything is energy, that everything has a certain vibration.

The Law of Attraction stipulates that like attracts like: vibrations that are alike will be attracted to each other like a magnet. This also means that a vibration that is different will be pushed away, it can't get close. *Positive* vibrations will attract more *positive* vibrations and *negative* vibrations will attract more *negative* vibrations.

We also saw in chapter 1 that our process begins with a thought. This thought has a certain vibration. Some thoughts are heavier, some are lighter. No thought is better than the other, it is just another kind of vibration. For example, everything on our planet needs to have a heavier vibration, otherwise it can't materialize in the first place. Or it will float up because it is too light to be held by gravity.

Since there is a lot of discussion about heavy and light energies (where heavy is bad and light is good), let's look at another example to show that none is better than the other. When we look at the different states of water, the concept may be clearer. In normal circumstances of air pressure (sea level) these are the states of water:

- Steam (gas): above 100 degrees Celsius
- Water (fluid): between 0 and 100 degrees Celsius
- Ice (solid): below 0 degrees Celsius

Is any of the three forms of water better than the other one? No, it is just another form with other characteristics and behaviors. Ice is heavier than water and water heavier than steam. One is more suited for one application than another. Or you could say that one is more suited to play a certain kind of game than another.

Like the Law of Gravity, the Law of Attraction works all the time. You can't neglect it, you can't undo it. It's just there all the time. It's also neutral—and has no judgment.

The Law of Gravity doesn't make a distinction between someone falling off a high building to his death or someone jumping from an airplane with a parachute with a safe landing. It's a law. It's neutral. It's objective. As human beings we may feel sorry for the first experience and admire the second one, but the Law of Gravity is indifferent to both.

The Law of Attraction is indifferent as well. Whether your vibrations attract experiences that human beings would call *positive* or *negative*, it doesn't matter. The Law of Attraction is also neutral.

What's *not* indifferent is your Higher Self. It always wants the best for you. So it helps you move towards joy. When something feels heavier to you, you are walking away from joy, and when it feels lighter, you are walking towards joy. However, it's up to you whether or not you listen to your Higher Power. You are still on the planet of Free Choice. Your Higher Self won't do things for you, It only supports you. And if you choose to ignore the signals It gives you, It will continue to bring you experiences so you can choose again.

How you can have the Law of Attraction work for you

Actually a better title would be: How to deal more consciously with the Law of Attraction. The Law of Attraction won't work more or less for you any more than the Law of Gravity will. However you can be more conscious of how the law works so you can receive more of what you desire.

The process of the Law of Attraction is a very simple one. These are the steps:

1. Ask
2. The Answer is Given
3. Allow

Let's look at the separate steps.

Step 1: Ask

Ask means asking for what you want. Asking for what you want to have, do or be. Asking for what you desire.

In the book *Ask and It is Given*, this first step is also called the step of deliberate creation.

You have probably read in a book, or heard others describe an exercise about writing down what you want in life. So I won't go into too many details, but will give you the basics.

So the first step is: writing down what you want in general terms.

For example,

I want to have:
- I want to have a nice car
- I want to have a beautiful house
- I want to have comfortable clothes

I want to do:
- I want to eat in a nice restaurant
- I want to go on a holiday
- I want to learn a new language

I want to be:
- I want to be good at playing basketball
- I want to be an interesting speaker
- I want to be a good partner
- I want to be in a nice relationship

Then the next step is to make it more specific.

For example,

I want to have:
- I want to have a new Audi A6 Allroad Quattro.
- I want to have a house with 4 bedrooms, 2 bathrooms, with a large garden, in a quiet street.
- I want to have a new pair of Levi's jeans, a Ralph Lauren shirt and Nike sneakers.

I want to do:
- I want to eat a 3-course dinner in a restaurant with at least 1 Michelin star for my birthday.
- I want to go on a two-week holiday to the sunny island of Crete.
- I want to take a Spanish course that is organized on a weekly basis in a nearby university.

I want to be:
- I want to be good at playing basketball: when playing a game I want to score 15 points and give 5 assists or more.
- I want to be an inspiring speaker: after each event 20 people or more send me a note via email, social media or the website to let me know how uplifting my speech was and how it changed the way they look at their lives.
- I want to be a loving and caring partner.
- I want to be in a harmonic relationship in which there is 'freedom in connectedness' (as free and centered individuals we choose to positively support each other and connect on a deep level).

What you notice is that there is no time element in those sentences. Like many other people I used to do goal-setting exercises using for example the SMART acronym. In such an exercise the goal should be:

- Specific
- Measurable
- Actionable / Acceptable
- Realistic
- Timely

Although this approach may be good for detailed tasks, it doesn't work so well for the important things in life. Using such a detailed approach limits the options and opportunities. Because in our Human Forms we only see a very small part of what is possible, we may miss out on ways or opportunities we hadn't thought of or that we didn't know existed. Adding a time element usually decreases our belief that it is possible to receive what we want. Especially when it is about the bigger dreams.

What are elements you can add?

- **Intensity.** The more burning your desire for one of the things you want, the more intense it is. The more intense, the more certain it is it will show up in your life.
- **Power**. The more you believe it is possible to receive what you asked for, the more certain it is it will show up in your life.
- **Duration**. The more you think about it and the longer you think about it, the more certain it is it will show up in your life.

The clue is to find the sweet spot. What is the sweet spot? It is the spot where your belief in what you want is 100% and your passion or intensity is very strong.

Some of the reasons why things you want don't show up in your life are:
- You want something, but actually you don't care that much about it. So the intensity is low. For example, a nice meal.
- You want something, but it seems so incredible. So your belief that you can have it is very low. For example, living in a castle.
- You did the exercise and you wrote something down, but you never thought about it anymore afterward. So the duration was very short.

Make sure that what you want is in the sweet spot.

What you will notice when you do this more often and experience some *successes* with it, is that some things that you want won't be that important anymore (their intensity decreases) and new ones appear in your mind. They're often larger than before, because your belief that you can have what you want has increased.

Other resources that help you attract what you want

There are a few fun ways to increase the intensity, power and duration.

Let's look at them and then you can choose which of them appeals to you and then you can start using it.

1. **Visualization**. Visualize receiving what you asked for. What does it look like? How does it feel? Use as many senses as you can. Getting as close to the physical manifestation as you can will help. For example, take a test drive with the car that you want. Visit the house you desire. Stand on the stage you want to perform on, etc.
2. **Dream book**. Use a notebook or a journal specifically purchased to write down all your dreams of the things, people and situations you want to experience in your life. Use a paper notebook with a pen.
3. **Vision board**. Use a corkboard or poster board on which you put images of everything you want. Cut the images out of magazines or find them on the Internet and print them. Then pin, or glue them on the board.

In other words: make it a game. Play with it and have fun !

Note: It's actually better to do an exercise like this by writing it down than imagining it in your head. It's better to do it with a pen on paper than doing it in a computer program like Microsoft Word. Why? The chances are higher that you'll actually receive what you desire. I haven't studied all the reasons why, but there are two reasons that I'm aware of:
1. *When you start writing things down, you will see where you missed an element. My personal experience has been, when I write things down I see where I jumped to conclusions or where I missed a crucial key to explain something.*
2. *When putting your thoughts and visions on paper (instead of in a document on your computer) you literally create a physical thing. Your thoughts become materialized: they become ink on paper, something tangible. Words in a document on your computer are still intangible. You can't physically grab them. It is like going from steam to water or ice. When water is steam it is sometimes hard to believe it is there, because you can't really touch it.*

After we have put what we want on paper, it is time for Step 2.

Step 2: The Answer is Given

In this step, your Higher Self looks at what you want. It is like your personal shopper ☺. It looks at your wish list (your 'shopping' list) and immediately starts working on it.

It asks other Higher Selves to play along and whisper in the ears of their Human Forms words that you need to hear. In cooperation with the other Higher Selves it creates situations for you.

Or to use game terminology: in this step the quests are created that you will encounter when you advance a little further in your game.

The good part about this step is that you don't have to do anything. Everything is done behind the curtains. Just as the character in the computer game doesn't need to know what the players are discussing or what the programmer is doing, neither do you. Even if you wanted to do something, you still couldn't do anything in this step, because this happens in a dimension you in your Human Form don't have a clue about.

Going back to the computer game analogy: the character in the game doesn't have a chat box, he is not even aware of its existence. The players are aware of it, but the character isn't.

So relax and let your Higher Self do all the work ☺.

Step 3: Allow

The third step goes back to you!

But again, good news! You don't have to DO anything. You just need to allow what you have requested to come to you. And that only requires being in your center, because that is the place where you don't resist what is coming.

It may sound weird when I write that you may resist what you have requested. The fact is you're not so much consciously resisting what you have been asking for. It's more that you're offering resisting thoughts. It's the broadcasting of a different vibration that keeps it away. In other words: if you are waiting for what you have asked for while being in Phase 1, or outpost energy, instead of being in your center, your 'order' will probably pass you by.

In order to bring you what you want, your Higher Self will conspire with other Higher Selves. In Step 2 they have thought about how they will present the fulfillment of your wishes to you and in this third step, it is materializing in the three-dimensional plane of space and time.

They will create events, they will send people towards you, they will put on television shows or a blog post with the information you need. Your Higher Self will whisper in your ear to buy a certain book, to follow a workshop, to watch a specific movie, to read a particular blog post, or to start a conversation with a stranger (who turns out to be an expert in the matter you are interested in).

To use the computer game analogy: the character in the computer game doesn't need to know what the players are discussing or what the programmer is doing. That is what happens in Step 2. In Step 3 the character just follows the commands of the player. It goes left when the player clicks left and right when the player clicks right. The big difference with human life is that in most computer games the character has less autonomy. But it doesn't matter just to make the point. I remember from the early days of computer games that there were text based adventure games where you could type in a command like "go left" where you got the answer "I can't go left." So it was up to me, as a player, to come up with a different solution. So I typed "Look left." The answer: "There is an impassable solid rock." New command: "Look right." Answer: "There is a door on the right." Command: "Open the door." Response: "The door is locked." Command: "Knock on the door." And so on and so on. This is what the interactive play of getting feedback and coming up with new solutions is like.

This is also what is happening when our Higher Self nudges us to go left by transmitting a light feeling in that direction and a heavy feeling in other directions. When we, in Human Form, ignore the nudge and decide to go right our Higher Self then needs to find another solution. From Its helicopter point of view It finds an alternative, without judging the choice you made. Once again it is up to you to follow or resist It's directions (feeling light or heavy). Do you listen to them or ignore them?

Our Higher Self is like a GPS system: it shows you the best way to reach your destination. Every time you decide to ignore its directions, it doesn't judge, but recalculates the route. It does that from its overview perspective (all the roads) mixed with live traffic information. However, you don't have to follow its directions, you can still do whatever you want.

Your Higher Self is giving you directions all the time. But if you are not in your center, you won't see the signs, hear the clues, attend the events, read the information, meet the people or hear what some of them say. When you are not centered you are at another wavelength, another vibration. To use an analogy that many personal and spiritual growth teachers use: you are tuned in to another radio station. You are tuned in to *Radio Complaint* at 100.00 FM. When you are tuned in to one radio station you can't hear what is being said on another one. You don't hear all the good stuff that is being shared on *The Effortless Living Channel* at 105.00 FM.

So how do you know you are on another wavelength?

Just listen to the signs your Higher Self gives you!

When it feels *heavy* then you are running away from the delivery from your 'order'. When it feels *light* you are running towards the delivery.

One of the most difficult things to do in this step is to trust that your Higher Self is taking care of your wish list in the best way possible. Many times this means that It will provide you with something larger, better, or more beautiful than you could have imagined or wished for. The pitfall is when you resist and restrict your Higher Power, then you miss the better thing. If your Higher Self is providing you with a Porsche, but you are still looking out for an Audi A6, you won't see it and you will miss the opportunity and the car.

The conversation may go like this:
- You: "Hey delivery boy. Yeah, you with that Porsche, go away from my driveway, I'm waiting for an Audi A6."
- Delivery boy: "But on my paper it says that this is the right address. It explicitly stated that I need to deliver this Porsche right here."
- You: "No, that's not what I ordered. Now, go away."

And then you are waiting and waiting for the Audi A6 to arrive. When it hasn't arrived many weeks later, you are disappointed that you haven't received your Audi A6 and you get angry with your Higher Self for not helping you ☺.

A famous story that has been around for a while and that is related to this topic is that of the priest who relies on God to be saved during a flood.

A terrible storm came into a town and local officials sent out an emergency warning that the riverbanks would soon overflow and flood the nearby homes. They ordered everyone in the town to evacuate immediately.

A faithful priest heard the warning and decided to stay, saying to himself, "I will trust God and if I am in danger, then God will send a divine miracle to save me."

The neighbors came by his house and said to him, "We're leaving and there is room for you in our car, please come with us!" But the priest declined. "I have faith that God will save me."

As the priest stood on his porch watching the water rise up the steps, a man in a canoe paddled by and called to him, "Hurry and come into my canoe, the waters are rising quickly!" But the priest again said, "No thanks, God will save me."

The floodwaters rose higher pouring water into his living room and the priest had to retreat to the second floor. A police motorboat came by and saw him at the window. "We will come up and rescue you!" they shouted. But the priest refused, waving them off saying, "Use your time to save someone else! I have faith that God will save me!"

The flood waters rose higher and higher and the priest had to climb up to his rooftop.

A helicopter spotted him and dropped a rope ladder. A rescue officer came down the ladder and pleaded with the priest, "Grab my hand and I will pull you up!" But the priest STILL refused, folding his arms tightly to his body. "No thank you! God will save me!"

Shortly after, the house broke up and the floodwaters swept the priest away and he drowned.

When in Heaven, the priest stood before God and asked, "I put all of my faith in You. Why didn't You come and save me?"

And God said, "Son, I sent you a warning. I sent you a car. I sent you a canoe. I sent you a motorboat. I sent you a helicopter. What more were you looking for?"

What we can learn from the example and the story, is that it is important to relax. Keep your eyes open and be open for whatever happens and trust that everything you desire will be given you in one way or the other. Don't be too attached to the specific outcome, but expect the outcome to be the best possible one for you.

It is much easier to do this when you are not living in your outpost the whole time. It is much easier when you are in your center! That is why there was so much emphasis on going from the outpost to the center in Chapters 2, 3 and 4.

More details about consciously working with the Law of Attraction

When working with the Law of Attraction, a lot of people (including me) had difficulties with applying it. Many people have questions and remarks about it, including:

- I know what I want, but it is not appearing in my life.
- I keep getting stuff I don't want. I keep getting situations, people and stuff in my life I didn't ask for.
- What happens when I don't desire anything?
- What happens when I (subconsciously) desire the wrong thing? And what about negative thoughts?
- Am I not asking too much? Don't I give my Higher Self too much work? Maybe I better ask only for the most important things?
- I have already received many things that I wished for in the past couple of weeks, but not that what I asked for two months ago. What is happening?
- I am in my center and open and I still don't seem to get what I want or at least not as fast as I want to have it.
- I feel quite overwhelmed and am inclining more towards a depression. I don't have much energy. As a consequence my desires are pretty low or in other words I don't care that much. I don't feel much passion for anything. What can I do?
- Most of the 'worldly' desires feel kind of meaningless to me, especially since I'm not playing the Phase 1 game anymore.

Let's look at these questions one by one.

I know what I want, but it is not appearing in my life.

Remember, the Law of Attraction works all the time.

If you want something, you give the signal to your Higher Self: bring more of this! If you don't want something, you give the signal to your Higher Self that you want something else. So actually it even doesn't matter that you don't always know exactly what you want. By acknowledging that you don't want something, your Higher Self gets the message that you want the opposite. That is how duality works.

The only problem is that we keep focusing on the things we don't want instead of on the opposite: what we do want. We keep focusing on our problems, and on the things that go wrong. In that way we are not in allowing modus. We are not in receiving modus. We are at another wavelength, listening to another radio station.

To put it differently: our Higher Self brings us what we want on the ground level, but we're still in the basement, complaining. Because we are yelling so hard at or about the things we don't want, we don't hear the courier with our order ringing the doorbell.

Other aspects and reasons why the Law of Attraction doesn't seem to work are:

- Is there still a feeling that you are not worthy of receiving what you desire?
- Are you getting overwhelmed by the how?
- How much do you believe that it is possible to receive something?

Is there still a feeling that you are not worthy of receiving what you desire?

If you still have a hard time believing that you can ask for anything, it may be worthwhile to go inside yourself and take an honest look: "Is there still something inside me that feels not worthy of receiving what I want?"

Be honest about it. Or do an exercise like the Focus Wheel Process to move up the emotional scale.

Getting overwhelmed by the how.

When we want something, a rather natural question to ask is: how is this going to happen?

The bigger something seems, the harder it is to imagine the ways it will come to you.

The pitfall here is to get fully immersed in the 'how' it will manifest, especially when past experiences showed you it wasn't possible. However, remember you were then in your outpost, playing the Phase 1 game. Now you have chosen another game, with other rules and other outcomes.

The good news is that you don't have to know the 'how' of how things manifest. That is part of Step 2. That is the responsibility of your Higher Self.

To be honest this is a hard one for me, especially because I'm very good at coming up with ways to do or achieve things ☺.
But the true process is about giving it over to your Higher Self, Who will figure out the how (Step 2), and focusing on being in the receiving mode (Step 3).

How much do you believe that it is possible to receive something?

It could also be that you already strongly believe that it is possible to attract something small, but that you don't believe you can attract something big (that's one I still have difficulties with sometimes ☺).

What you can do is start with what you believe can happen. An example that is used a lot (and that I also used to start with) is that of attracting a parking spot.

How does the exercise go?

Next time you have to go to a party, or out to eat, either by yourself or with friends, go into your center and ask your Higher Self for a parking spot near the place. If you feel confident enough, ask for a spot right in front of the door, otherwise use a 100 meter radius. It is important to keep believing that you will get it. If you have never done this exercise before, your wicked warriors will probably intervene and tell you it's not possible. Embrace them and go back to your center. Also when other people tell you that it will be impossible to find a parking spot up close because it is a very crowded place, stay in your center. It also helps to not be attached to the result. If a *must* comes in, you know your wicked warriors are playing their game again. However, if you can stay relaxed and trust the Universe to act for you, your parking spot will be there!

After doing this a couple of times you will notice that your trust in the process has increased. Your belief has increased. Now you can start attracting other things you may have believed to be out of your league. For example, a car, a new job, a relationship, a house, etc.

Another way of not believing something, is to mentally want it, but not emotionally feel it. Words are but a small part of the way we ask and desire things. Desires emanate from within (they are kind of a feeling without any words describing them). Desires then become ideas, then words. This happens so quickly in our minds we're often not aware of it. Sometimes our words don't match our feelings. Chances are that you have already wished for something in your life—whether you knew about the Law of Attraction or not – and that you didn't receive it.

Most of the time we fail to receive is because we use the words, "I would like to have a new Mercedes," but we don't really believe that that is possible. When we look at our bank account, we only see enough money to barely pay all our bills. So our words say, "I would like to have a new car," but at the same time the voice in our mind says, "That's impossible. It can't happen now and it won't ever happen." As a result we feel bad and tune in to *Radio Complaint* and we never hear the *Effortless Living Channel* playing our song!

How do we deal with this situation?

We find the sweet spot.

For example's sake, let's use this situation: John voices as a desire, "I would like to have a new Mercedes." He doesn't believe that this is possible because he even can't pay the current bills.

This is what I would recommend John to do, using the train analogy:

Step 1: if your train is moving in the *negative* direction, it is important to slow it down first so it can come to a stop, before you reverse it and head off in the *positive* direction.

- John, realize that you are in your outpost and not in your center.
- *If necessary apply one of the tips from previous chapters to move to your center. For example, use EFT (Emotional Freedom Techniques).*
- John, look at your wish and your thoughts and feelings. What seems to be the case is that you are now more focused on having just enough money to pay the bills. So let's rephrase your desire for now to, "I would like to have enough money to pay the bills some day." (general expression).
- Do you believe it is possible to have enough money to pay the bills some day?
- John: "Yes."
- How much on a scale from 1 (totally impossible) to 10 (I'm totally confident that this is going to happen) do you believe this?
- John: "I'd say a 9".
- How do you feel?
- John: "Less stress. Less resistance."

So by making your expression more general you will slow down the train moving in the *negative* direction. There will be less stress and less resistance. The wicked warriors will be arguing and interfering less.

Step 2: now let's turn the train in a *positive* direction by making a general statement in the *positive* direction.

- John, let's assume that you have enough money to pay the bills. Can you do that?
- John: "Yes"
- How are you feeling now?
- John: "Calm."
- OK, let's use another phrase: "Now that I have paid all my bills, I would like to have more money." How does that feel?
- John: "That feels OK."
- How much on a scale from 1 (totally impossible) to 10 (I'm totally confident that this is going to happen) do you believe this?
- John: "I'd say about an 8."

Step 3: since we are moving in a *positive* direction now, let's speed things up.

- John, let's assume you have some money left after you paid all the bills. Can you do that?
- John: "Yes"
- How are you feeling now?
- John: "Good."
- OK, let's use another phrase: "Now I have some money left, I may save some money to buy a new car some day." How does that feel?
- John: "Actually, I'm getting excited a little bit ☺."
- How much on a scale from 1 (totally impossible) to 10 (I'm totally confident that this is going to happen) do you believe this?
- John: "Definitely an 8."

Step 4: let's speed it up some more.

- John, let's assume you have saved some money. Can you do that?
- John: "Yes."
- How are you feeling now?
- John: "Enthusiastic."
- OK, let's use another phrase: "I would like to buy a new Mercedes." How does that feel?
- John: "My stomach shrinks."
- How much on a scale from 1 (totally impossible) to 10 (I'm totally confident that this is going to happen) do you believe this?
- John: "No more than a 3."
- What happened?
- John: "Well, a Mercedes is a very expensive car. I don't know if I can ever save enough money to buy such a car. And even if I would have saved some money, I may want to buy some new clothes or go on a holiday as well."
- OK, but could you still buy a new car, but a cheaper one?
- John: "Yes, of course."

So what happened here, is that we have found John's sweet spot is about buying a new car. Not a Mercedes. A Mercedes is too far removed from his current vibrational point, at least for now. Because John is now in a place of non-resisting and when he doesn't go back looking at his current situation while tuning in to *Radio Complaint*, chances are high that he will get some ideas or proposals from people through which his financial situation will improve. He will probably say: "You can't believe what happened, I got a promotion at work. And I also won a new car with a local lottery. Wow, such a coincidence. I'm very lucky."

At the same time his Higher Self is smiling brightly because It had been orchestrating events like this for a while because the only thing It wants to do is assist John in being happy and joyful. But John hadn't paid attention to his Higher Self's clues, hadn't listened to the people who were sent by his Higher Self, and hadn't taken action on any of the ideas he received. However, just by releasing resistance, everything fell into place, and even quicker than John could ever have imagined.

Note: if you want to use the train analogy, these are the elements:

- In order to go in the other direction, first slow down, then stop, reverse, speed up and then go full throttle.
- Slowing down = making wishes more general. You will feel more relief and less resistance.
- Speeding up = making wishes more specific. You will feel more excited.

This is one of the reasons I didn't see consistent results. When I wanted something 'negative' in my life to change, I created specific thoughts about positive changes. What happened: more shocks, because I was switching the full speed trigger from going backward to going forward. The passengers (my emotions and the world around me) were shaken up. Because that didn't feel good, I created more negative thoughts and got caught up in the Phase 1 game again.

It is also good to know that the physical manifestation is only in the last few percentages of the 3-Step Law of Attraction process. When it manifests, it is already complete. However, most people first have to see things with their own eyes before they can start believing something is possible. In the meantime they are listening to *Radio Complaint* and are missing all the clues and hints from their Higher Self that is broadcasting at the Effortless Living Channel.

I keep getting stuff I don't want. I keep getting situations, people and stuff in my life I didn't ask for. What is going on?

The answer to this question is an extension to the previous one. So read the explanation in the previous question first (if you haven't done so already).

Then ask yourself these questions:

- Where are you: in the outpost or in your center?
- What are you focusing on? Probably you are giving more attention to the things you don't want than the things you do want.

- Did you also notice the good things that have happened in the meanwhile? Did you see that you received some things that you wanted as well, as small as they may be?

Most of the time people who experience things they don't want, are still playing the Phase 1 game. As already mentioned, the focus in the outpost is on attack/defense. In other words, the focus is on things you want to avoid, not the things you want to attract. And even when the things you want show up, you don't always believe it can be true: "It must be like a Trojan horse. Something bad will happen soon."

That's why it is important to move from the outpost to the center first. It's easy to receive the things you want from your center. And you won't experience things you don't want so much anymore.

A way to shift that focus is to start paying attention to the good things that ARE happening. Maybe they're not the things you explicitly want, but you will definitely notice that many good things are happening around you. And don't look at just your own life. Notice what happens in the lives of the people around you. If your neighbor tells you that he has just gotten an unexpected promotion, this is a sign. Because you are aware of it, it came into your energy field. So instead of being jealous that he has all the good luck, be happy. Good things are coming your way as well.

Look at it like you would look at the first beams of the sun in the morning. They're small. You probably don't feel the warmth of the sun yet. But you know that the sun is coming up and that you will definitely will feel its warmth later on. You don't doubt it's going to happen. You don't lock yourself in your basement and start complaining that there is no sun. You patiently wait, knowing the sun is on its way! In other words: start looking for the signs that the good stuff is coming your way and anticipate with joy that it is coming!

What happens when I don't desire anything?

Actually that is not possible.

On this planet of duality, we are making choices the whole time: I want this and I don't want that. We don't even have to speak about the situations, people or objects at hand. We always have our thoughts about them.

Wanting something or having a preference is not the same as judging something. Judging includes labeling something as *right* or *wrong*. Choosing (or having a preference) doesn't include that.

For example, when you go to a buffet in a restaurant, you may choose prawns and not the chicken. Next time (or next round ☺) you may choose the chicken and not the prawns. It's about choice. Or on Monday you decide to wear a blue sweater and on Tuesday a red one. It's not that you deem the blue one better than the second. At a certain moment you just have another preference.

So at anytime you are choosing something, your Higher Self takes note of that. It takes note of both what you want and what you don't want. Then it will make sure that you will receive more of what you want and less of what you don't want. It gives you clues where to find what you want: whenever you have a lighter feeling, you are closer to something you want. Whenever the feeling gets heavier, you are moving away from it.

What happens when I (subconsciously) desire the wrong thing? And what about negative thoughts?

Ah. This is a part that so many people are afraid of from the moment they have learned about the Law of Attraction.

First you can always choose again. It is not that you specifically can 'undo' something, but you can just choose something else. This is a very important part to understand. Many people are striving to keep as many unwanted things out of their life as possible. They hope to only attract the *good stuff* in this way.

However, there are two big problems with this:

1. Since the world is changing at such a rapid pace, you don't know which unwanted thing will show up when or where. As a consequence you need to be on guard the whole time.
2. Your focus is on the things you don't want instead of what you do want.

For example, let's assume you are on holiday with a friend in Spain and need to drive from Madrid to Barcelona. He is the driver and you are the navigator.

Scenario A: you are constantly watching out for directions so you don't go in the wrong direction.
- You start driving and suddenly you see a sign: Burgos, Zaragoza, Bilbao, Santander, Pamplona, Valladolid, Leon, Santiago de Compostela left. Barcelona right.
- Since you are the navigator, you need to look at the signs and tell your friend where to go. So in your mind you are going:
  - Burgos: no, that's no good.
  - Zaragoza: no, that's no good.
  - Bilbao: no, that's no good.

- Your friend: "Which direction should I take?"
- You keep going:
  - Santander: no, that's no good.
  - Pamplona: no, that's no good.
- Your friend, who is getting a little agitated says: "Which direction do I take?"
- You keep going:
  - Valladolid: no, that's no good.
  - Leon: no, that's no good.
- Since it is taking so long, your friend starts yelling: "I need your answer RIGHT NOW!"
- Because you haven't found a right answer yet, you say: "Turn left!" reasoning that is the best direction simply because there are the most cities that way and Barcelona will probably be one of them.

In other words: since you were so focused on the places to avoid, it took you a long time to read and sift through which way to go. This caused you to doubt which direction to take, so you ended up getting off of the wrong exit anyway.

Scenario B: you are watching out for directions to go in the right direction.

- You start driving and suddenly you see a sign: Burgos, Zaragoza, Bilbao, Santander, Pamplona, Valladolid, Leon, Santiago de Compostela left. Barcelona right.
- You scan the sign for the direction you want. And see that Barcelona is to the right.
- Your friend asks: "Which direction to take?"
- You answer: "Right."

In other words: since you didn't care about all the other options. When you focused only on the thing you did want, life suddenly became a lot easier!

The good news is that you can always switch from scenario A to scenario B, even when you are already on the road. You don't have to go back to Madrid once you have taken the wrong exit. You can also take the next exit with the sign to Barcelona or in the direction of Barcelona.

Let's use the buffet analogy again: you just choose from the buffet what you want. You don't ask the waiters to remove the items from the buffet that you don't want.

In other words: success with the Law of Attraction is about focusing on what you want instead of what you are trying to avoid.

Secondly, what about negative thoughts?

When people learn about the Law of Attraction, they are worried about any *negative* thoughts they may have.

They have learned: *positive* vibrations will attract more *positive* vibrations and *negative* vibrations will attract more *negative* vibrations. So now they are worried that their *negative* thoughts will attract more *negative* thoughts. As I have already shared: if you choose 'wrong', the good news is that you always can choose again. You can always choose something different.

The greatest relief may be that not everything happens instantaneously. Although manifestations happen faster and faster, there is still a delay between your thoughts and the actual manifestation of something. In other words: it is not because you have a *negative* thought, that all hell will break loose in a moment.

How does it work?

According to the *Teachings of Abraham*, within 17 seconds of focusing on something, a matching vibration becomes activated. So it will start to attract similar thoughts. However, the vibration won't have much attraction power yet. It is only when you manage to stay purely focused upon any thought for 68 seconds that the vibration will be powerful enough for the manifestation to begin. In other words you still have enough time to choose a less resistant thought in the meanwhile!

On the other hand it also explains something else. When we are in our outpost we are vigilant for potential attacks. Because our focus is the whole time on possibly being attacked, we will attract thoughts and events that reinforce that belief. And we will see the manifestation of it in one way or the other.

So again, the invitation is to go from your outpost to your center. Life from your center is a lot quieter, plus either your attack/defense thoughts won't show up, or you'll catch them quickly.

Even when you are in your outpost, you can change things. Some personal or spiritual growth teachers say that a positive thought is 10 times stronger than a negative thought. My internal response to hearing that for the first time was: "Man, I still have so many negative thoughts, more than 10 times as much as positive ones, so I'm still very worried about my life." Isn't that another great trick of the wicked warriors? ☺

Grasping another analogy also helped me. The river of Well-Being always flows. So it isn't necessary to only offer positive thoughts (paddling downstream). The only thing that matters is to release the oars a bit when paddling upstream. Why? The moment you stop paddling upstream, the river will take your boat and turn it in the other direction (downstream).

In other words, just finding a little relief is enough. You don't have to stop all negative thoughts; you don't have to only think positive thoughts. Just releasing a few negative thoughts is enough. When we don't focus on the negative and we arrive at a more neutral position, there are no roadblocks for our Higher Self to deliver what we wanted. And we don't offer any resistance in receiving it anymore either.

Am I not asking too much? Am I not giving my Higher Self too much work? Maybe I'd better ask only for the most important things?

The good news is that you never can ask for too much. Contrary to what you may believe, there is no lack in the Universe, nor in the world. However when you look at the world from a Phase 1 perspective there is lots of evidence of a lack in the world. That perception alone is enough reason to attack or defend. But is that perception true?

For example, when you look at the oil reserves, you will see that they are finite. There is not an abundant, ever-flowing supply of oil. However, the question is: what do we need? Do we need oil? Or do we need energy? I assume that you agree with me that it is the latter. Nowadays, there are lots of alternatives for oil, even free energy. Actually, there are already technological solutions for most of the perceived lack of resources on this planet. So we truly can all live together in peace. "So what are we waiting for?" you may ask. My answer at this moment in time is: we are only waiting for enough people to go from their outpost to their center so there are enough examples and experiences for the rest of the world about how life can be experienced. I hope to make a contribution to that belief system with this book. However, I know the greatest contribution I can make, is to live from my center as much as possible. And I hope you will accept my invitation to do that as well!

Please stay vigilant for the little, more subtle monsters that are still there. I know several people who perceive themselves as very spiritual and at the same time are writing or speaking about "Stop the war!" or "Say no to drugs!" Others say: "No more child labor!" or "Eliminate world hunger." While you may applaud those initiatives, I invite you to take a step back and realize what is happening most of the time there:

1. They perceive a specific group of people as victims. Or at least they think they are the rescuers or saviors, which makes those people victims anyway. So they are playing the victim-savior/rescuer game.
2. They are focusing their thoughts and their vibrations **against** something. It means that they are vibrating at a level of something they don't want. Because like attracts like, they will have more similar thoughts. That will keep them in a negative vibration (which makes it hard to attract a positive solution) or

provide them with thoughts, ideas and evidence that reinforce their belief. And as a consequence fuels their battle.

Am I saying to stop all initiatives to change the world? No, on the contrary!

I invite everyone to first look very honestly at what is going on. For example,

"Why am I supporting this initiative?"

- Do you see those people as victims? Do you see yourself as a rescuer or savior?
- If not, why are you doing this? Is it because of your perception that there is lack somewhere?

"Can we change the focus? Can we decide what we want to go **for** instead of **against**?"

- Instead of wanting to "eliminate world hunger," let's change the initiative to "food for every person in the world."
- Always be vigilant: if the name would be changed to "feed every person in the world" we would still be making ourselves rescuers and other people victims.
- What words are being used in a campaign or on a website? If there are still many attack/defense words like eliminate, destroy, annihilate, fight, safeguard, protect, secure, shield, etc. there is still a lot of fear-based energy.

"Am I attached to a specific result?"

- If you are working towards "food for every person in the world," does it matter what food it is? How many meals a day? Can you set aside your opinion what it must look like and trust that it may even be better?

In other words: I would like to invite everyone to look for his or her center first. From the outpost no solutions will be found. And then look deeply inside: is there still some lack, some hole that needs to be filled? Or are you doing this to extend only Love? Are you trusting that the best thing will happen? Or do you feel the need to fix something?

Let's go back to the questions: Am I not asking too much? Am I not giving my Higher Self too much work? Maybe I 'd better ask only for the most important things?

So you already know there is no lack. This also means: it's not because you ask for something that someone else can't have it. Or it's not that because it doesn't exist yet, it can't be created.

Let me share the example of a friend of mine, Christoph.

A few years ago Christoph wanted to change careers within his company. He wanted to go from the sales and marketing department to the training department. Unfortunately, at that time there was no job opening. That didn't stop him. He kept educating himself and envisioned that he would get such a job without having to change companies.

A few months later, suddenly there was a job opening. Christoph applied and due to the specific job profile, there were only two candidates. It was clear that with his skills and experience he would be the best fit for that job (which was also confirmed by his mentors in the company). However due to—let me call it—internal politics, the other person got the job. Christoph was very disappointed, and very angry at first.

Again that didn't stop him. He looked at what the positive key learning could be and he realized that the job would have been very interesting, but that it was not the perfect one for him. There were several parameters and personal values missing.

Once he realized that, he adapted his plan and started envisioning his dream job, the one that would be the perfect fit for him. The only detail was that this kind of role didn't exist in the company he worked for.

Nevertheless, he envisioned himself in this job every day. He took on projects outside his current function, but within his circle of influence, in order to bring about the change in the company to create his dream job. One year later the leadership team was really impressed with Christoph's actions and vision. They realised the company needed more of this. A new role and a new job was created, exactly the one Christoph had envisioned.

By specifically formulating his wishes, fine-tuning them and visualizing them, Christoph gave a clear message to his Higher Self. His Higher Self accepted his wish list and something was created that nobody had ever imagined possible.

In the non-physical realm, where your Higher Self resides, there is no need to sleep in order to have the body refreshed. In fact, your Higher Self is waiting for you to ask for help, inspiration, to set things in motion. Because you in your Human Form are an extension of your Higher Self, it is more than happy to support you. The more you experience, the more It experiences. The more joy you feel, the more joy It feels.

Actually you may even say that your Higher Self not only fully wants to help you all the time, you kind of deprive It from having experiences when you don't.

So you can always ask, it will never be too difficult or too much!

172

I have to be honest here. A part that I still have some difficulties with myself is about the magnitude of what I'm asking for. I have experienced that from my three-dimensional perspective it seems easier to attract a nice meal than an eight-bedroom house. It still seems as if it is much harder to get the house than the meal. But that's because I look from a perspective of how much time, work or money needs to be put into something in this three-dimensional world of space and time.

On planet Earth it takes more time, energy, work and money to build a house than to prepare a meal. Although I have had some kind of confirmation of the fact that it doesn't matter what you ask for, after all my first two books became best sellers, I have to admit that this challenge is one that I still have difficulties with myself. But don't let this limiting belief stop **you**! ☺

To recapitulate: you can never ask too much and you can ask for anything, no matter how big or small it is.

I am in my center and very open, yet I still don't seem to get what I want, or at least not as fast as I want it.

Let's rephrase this: even when you are in receiving mode, when you are in your center, you don't seem to get what you have asked for. Or at least you haven't received it yet, or it takes longer to arrive than expected.

One of two things may be going on.

1. You may be taking the scenic route.
2. There is still some doubt. Your wicked warriors are still present.

When going from place A to place B, the fastest route may be the highway. However, when you hike or bike you may enjoy the scenery much more.

So give it an honest look: what is most important for you here? To arrive at your destination as fast as possible? To get what you asked for as quickly as possible?

Or are you presented with an opportunity to enjoy the ride? To enjoy the scenery? To fully experience what is going on? Maybe part of receiving is being able to realize what was needed to provide you with what you wanted so you could be more grateful?

If you do the exercise with attracting the parking spot and you did everything right and still didn't get one, look for what has happened. Instead of parking your car in a 100-meter radius, you are now parked 200 meter away. What happened on your walk to your destination is that you encountered someone who needed directions. After you helped him out, he gave you big smile that warmed your heart. As a consequence you arrive at the party in a joyful mood. The energy you radiated was noticed by another guest, which led into a nice conversation and a wonderful date a week later!

In a previous question there was a concern about *negative* things. The same principles apply to *positive* things. Every time we have a *positive* thought, but don't hang on to it, it loses its power to attract more *positive* thoughts or feelings. But actually, not hanging on to positive thoughts is not a big problem either since it is our natural state to attract joyful experiences. The problem is that we switch back to negative thoughts: "The parking space is never going to happen. I will have to drive around for 30 minutes and then the nearest parking spot I will find is more than 500 meters away."

It's like your Higher Self was already on Its way with your shopping list to the Heavenly Grocery Store, but then you lost your focus or changed your mind. "Ah, apparently (s)he doesn't want it anymore, needs to rethink it or wants something else, so I'll return home and await the new list." That's how your Higher Self responds to your thoughts. In the parking spot example: "Ah, he changed his mind. Instead of a parking spot in front of the door, he now wants to drive 30 minutes around and park at 500 meters distance. OK, I will give the parking spot in front of the door then to someone else and will create the experience he wants."

If the above is not the case and you still haven't received what you want, you may have encountered another level of fear, doubt or worry.

The more monsters you have turned into teddy bears, the less there are left. So, you'll have fewer monsters left, but they'll be much harder to see since they are smaller and more subtle. You won't see or recognize them immediately. However, the good news is that since they are much smaller, they are less frightening and thus much easier to look at and transform into teddy bears.

So give things a decent and honest look: is there still some Phase 1 game that is being played? Is there still a monster crying for help to be transformed?

174

I have already received many things that I wished for in the past couple of weeks, but not that what I asked for two months ago. What is happening?

Your Higher Self doesn't mind the magnitude of what you want. And it also doesn't take the order of your list into account. It doesn't work according to the FIFO (First In First Out) principle ☺.

Since It has a helicopter overview It sees more clearly what would be best for you and when. On the other hand, not all resources may be available at the same time.

For me the image of the Heavenly Game Room explains this very clearly.

Assume that you have asked for a new partner. Your Higher Self looks around and sees that Kim would be the best match for your request. When asking Kim's Higher Self about Kim's availability to play the relationship game with you, It answers: "What a marvelous idea! One problem, Kim is currently in another relationship. So give me some time to make Kim available to have the experience with your Human Form in the three-dimensional realm. Wow, this looks like so much fun! I'm already looking forward to it. In the meantime we can start planning how they will meet each other. Let's have them meet at work." So your Higher Self knows that it will take a little while before Kim is available, but It starts orchestrating events so your organization attracts a new client, namely the company Kim works for.

So you may say: "Well, good things have been happening lately. One of them is that we attracted a new client. Actually, that went pretty fast, I just asked my Higher Self for it last week. However I'm still waiting for a new relationship. I placed that order a while ago, when will it come?"

It is coming, but it hasn't shown up in your life yet. To use the computer game analogy again: it hasn't shown up on your Mini Map yet. But it is there. Trust your Higher Self and focus on being in *allowing* mode while you wait.

I feel quite overwhelmed and am leaning towards depression. I don't have much energy. As a consequence my desires are pretty low. In other words I don't care that much. I don't feel much passion for anything. What can I do?

First, in this situation, as far as I know people are either in their outpost or they are in their center, but not consciously connected with their Higher Self. The explanation for the second situation will be given in the next chapter of the book.

How to deal with the first situation? Actually, it comes down to feeling good. Or at least feeling a little bit better, feeling some relief.

These are steps you can take. You can do all of them in the order below, or just one or a few of them, in the order you want. It's totally up to you. Isn't that nice? There's so much freedom! ☺

- Realize you are in your outpost. Sometimes this is already enough to see and feel differently.
- Pick one or more of the tips from Chapter 2 to relax the wicked warriors.
- Use the Focus Wheel Process to move up the Emotional Guidance Scale. Remember that it doesn't have to be perfect; you just want to feel a little bit better. You can also use another tool or technique from Chapter 3.
- Your belief in attracting good things is probably low. Most of the time the cause is a lot of doubt: since you can't see how your current situation can change, you don't believe it will. What can help is to wish for something general. Using the train analogy: slow down the *negative* part first before you start speeding up in the *positive* direction. For example, "I feel OK." Do this before saying "I feel excellent." Only ask for specific, *positive* stuff after you feel more neutral.

Most of the *worldly* desires feel kind of meaningless to me, especially since I'm not playing the Phase 1 game anymore.

Actually, that's good news! That means you are ready for the next chapter! ☺

Chapter 6: The Game of Joyful Connected Living

Until now, we have seen that you can live life according to the Phase 1 game (in the outpost) or the centered Phase 2 game.

In this chapter we will take the next step: play the Phase 3 game.

However, Phase 3 not for everybody. At least, not yet ☺.

When you are still immersed in the Phase 1 game most of the time, you may find this part of the book hard to believe or relate to. If that is the case, I kindly invite you to park your doubts or judgment about it and focus first on getting more out of your outpost and into your center.

When you are in your center, come back to this chapter. That may take a few days, a few months, or maybe a few years. The length of time it takes doesn't matter. Please know that when you eventually make your way back here, you'll say, "How could I have missed this? How could I have rejected this? How could I have skipped that chapter? If I had known this information sooner, my life would have been much different."

How do I know this is likely to happen? Because it happened to me ☺. Not with this book of course, but with others, like *A Course In Miracles,* the *Teachings of Abraham* and the *Way of Mastery* series. The first time I delved into that information I was not in the right place to receive it. Only after I was more centered, was I really able to grasp what was written there. The more I'm in my center, the more I understand what those books really are about. And my understanding grows deeper every day. I already shared with you the fact that I will stay a student, and I hope you do as well ☺.

To take the next step and move into Phase 3, more willingness is required. The willingness, and hence the decision to look for alignment with your Higher Self and to live from that alignment, is necessary to move forward.

"Why should I want to do that?" you may ask.

First, because the more you are aligned, the smoother everything in your daily life in this Human Form on this three-dimensional planet of space and time will go. You will have less resistance and less hard work to do. Everything will feel lighter and more effortless. Remember, your Higher Self is guiding you. That Self has the helicopter view. It sees the 'blocks on the road' on the one hand and the opportunities on the other hand.

Secondly, because you will find the answers to why you are here on the planet. You will find your individuated form of bringing *light* to the world. In general we are all here to bring *light* to the world. But there are so many ways to do that. We already saw that everybody's path to find and embrace his or her shadows/fears is different. Well, the same applies to bringing *light* to the world as well. When you are connected to your Higher Self, you will be inspired by all the ways you can bring your piece of the puzzle to the world. And by bringing your piece of the puzzle to the world, you'll inspire other people to do the same. Because you can't ask or demand that people bring their *light,* you can only inspire them by being the example.

You can bring your piece of the puzzle to the world in different areas in your life as well. Some prefer to do it in their professional field, others via their hobby. Other people do it 'in between', bringing it when they meet people on the street, on the bus or while waiting in line at a shop. Just giving someone a genuine smile while you are centered and connected may change someone's day, or even their lives. For example: people who were thinking about attempting suicide changed their mind because someone waved, or smiled or acknowledged them with a smile.

When you start to live more and more from the place of a centered connection, you will experience that the worldly matters like a house, a car, a job or even a relationship will start to change. They will have less and less power over you. You will find yourself less and less attached to them. This will give you the freedom to be more and more yourself and radiate your *light,* whether or not others see it.

When you are in your outpost or when you are in your center but not consciously connected to your Higher Self, you'll always have a hope that through your house, car, job or relationship you will be seen as valuable. Because you are still identified with them, this can cause pain when your well-intended actions are not seen or you are rejected. But when you are consciously connected to your Higher Self, it doesn't matter anymore. You will no longer be attached to the result. And when you are really in that spot of freedom, after a while you will experience that there will be no rejection as long as you can remain centered. The people who ignored you or rejected you either won't do that anymore, or they will have disappeared from your life.

When you are still in your outpost or not consciously connected to your Higher Self, it may be hard to imagine this. Chances are your current relationship, or the person you are secretly in love with, means the world to you. You couldn't imagine living without them. But when you are consciously connected to your Higher Self, that feeling will change. You can still be with them, but you don't *need* them anymore. The relationship will be a deliberate choice from both sides. As a consequence the relationship will go from 'special' to 'holy'. 'Special' means that there is a need in you that you can't fill, so you want the other person to fill that hole for you. 'Holy' means that both you and the relationship are whole: nothing needs to be changed or fulfilled.

178

That ultimate fulfillment will become like the beautifully worded description in the book *The Way of Knowing*:

"The holy relationship is the relationship between any two who choose to look upon each other, having looked within and found no lack. For those two can then look out upon one another and see only perfect innocence, only perfect peace, only perfect Love."

In other words: the basis for any good relationship is freedom.

Likewise, when you are struggling with money, the relationship you have with your finances will change when you are consciously connected to your Higher Self. You will be guided in directions about how to avoid financial distress and where to find monetary abundance. However, this is something that cannot be forced. When I read sentences like this when I was still in my outpost, I used my will and lots of energy to try to make financial abundance happen. I used the Law of Attraction and was kind of successful, only to find myself looking for other forms of acceptance. I created a big shield around myself to avoid rejection. This cost me a lot of energy, and led to a minor burnout. (Or at least I think it was minor, I was too caught up in the Phase 1 game to notice ☺).

In other words: the move from the outpost to the center is crucial in order to have a good foundation to continue to build upon. Once you are in your center, and consciously connected with your Higher Self (even if it's just once in a while), you will see that your financial situation and relationships will improve as well. That improvement will be a consequence of being guided. It comes about as a result of not working against the natural flow of well being. The natural flow of well being is what contains amongst other things, abundant money and successful relationships.

Of course nobody is forced to take the steps from the outpost to the center and from the center to being consciously connected to their Higher Selves. We're still living on a planet of free will. However taking these steps will provide you with many of the answers to the questions you might have regarding your life:

- Why am I here?
- How can I make a meaningful contribution?
- What is the sense of it all?
- What is my purpose?
- Why should I live and not commit suicide?

I can share some of the insights I have received. However, you will probably find the ones YOU really need to hear or read only when you are consciously connected with your Higher Self.

In general, from my experience, the answers to these popular questions are generally along these lines:

- **Why am I here?** To experience joy in a Human Form, to create (inspired by your Higher Self) and to extend Love.
- **How can I make a meaningful contribution?** You are here to shine your light, and to inspire others by being the living example of what life looks like when you are consciously connected with your Higher Self. When you are following the directions of your Higher Self, the specifics of your life will reveal themselves.
- **What is the sense of it all?** To heal separation and to experience Oneness again.
- **What is my purpose?** To bring light and love to the world. It's also to experience the joy that is the result of that love and light.
- **Why should I live and not commit suicide?** Because you are a unique part of the puzzle. Without you the puzzle won't be whole. Without you bringing your spark of light, there will always be something missing. Of course you have the freedom, and the free will or choice to do what you want—even if that choice means choosing to step out of this current life. However, you will be back in a Human Form till you have decided that you will bring your light. So why not do it now, in this lifetime? (At least that's how I look at it ☺).

When you read words like, "being an example to others," or "inspiring other people," you may feel scared or overwhelmed. What may be happening is that you are reminded of the enormous power you possess. You may feel that you have abused this power in this lifetime or a previous one. However, if you are using your power from a centered position, and are consciously connected with your Higher Self, you can't abuse it.

That is what Nelson Mandela referred to when he quoted Marianne Williamson from her book, *Return to Love*:

> "Our deepest fear is not that we are inadequate. Our deepest fear is that we are powerful beyond measure. It is our light, not our darkness that most frightens us. We ask ourselves, who am I to be brilliant, gorgeous, talented, and fabulous? Actually, who are you not to be? You are a child of God. Your playing small does not serve the world. There is nothing enlightened about shrinking so that other people will not feel insecure around you. We are all meant to shine, as children do. We were born to make manifest the glory of God that is within us. It is not just in some of us; it is in everyone and as we let our own light shine, we unconsciously give others permission to do the same. As we are liberated from our own fear, our presence automatically liberates others."

I can imagine that you still feel afraid to shine your light. Remember that you are not alone. Actually, when you are really connected to your Higher Self, you won't feel alone anymore. Even when there is no other person around, you won't feel separated. You will feel your connection with Oneness. You won't feel alone, but 'all-one'. What will happen then is new people will come into your life—people who are also living from their center and in connection with their Higher Self.

Things may be awkward in the beginning because you don't know how to approach them. But just recognizing each other is often enough to spark your connection. You will recognize them as one who has decided that it is time to shine their light. And they will recognize you. Just by seeing the sparkle in each other's eyes you are reminded that life is good and that you are an excellent ambassador of bringing light and love to the world!

What may be keeping you from 'buying into this' is that when you look out into the world, you see other people. They seem separate from you. That is indeed what it looks like on the three-dimensional planet of space and time. However two words have been mixed up: separation and individuation. We believe we are separate from everything (and when we are in the outpost the wicked warriors are continually providing evidence of that). However, our life here is not about separation, but individuation. It is about playing a unique game while being connected to all the rest.

To use a metaphor from the *Way of Mastery* series: the Universe and all the life in it, is like an ocean. On top of the ocean are waves. Although they have the same characteristics of the ocean and are continuously connected to it, you can point to them as individual waves. You can do that till they have washed ashore and retreated back into the sea, and then they become part of the ocean again.

In our Human Form, we are the waves. We're on top of the ocean. Each of us has a different, individual layer of foam and a unique appearance. At the same time we are a part of the ocean—we are not separated from it. We are each a crucial part of the ocean, otherwise it wouldn't be the ocean anymore. Now, let's assume there is a first layer under the wave that is not visible when you are standing on the beach. That is our Higher Self. It is our connection to the rest of the ocean, to the rest of the Universe. So you can compare your current life with a wave from the ocean, which starts at one point and ends on the beach. When it washes ashore, the ocean absorbs it again. It is not gone; it is just reabsorbed before forming another wave, or another life.

This chapter of the book is about feeling the connection with the ocean, with the Universe, with God, via your Higher Self. And when you feel that connection, there will be more peace. There will be less to worry about. And at the same time you also will be in touch with Life Energy much more. You will feel it inside of you and feel it radiate through you. And you will feel joy like you may never have felt joy before.

The more you make the decision to live life from your center in connection with your Higher Self, the easier, more effortlessly and lighter your life will become. And you will be an en-light-ened being.

The funny part is that I — and many other people — have been brought up with the concept of Heaven as a 'place' we go to after our physical body has passed away. We've been taught that when you are enlightened you don't have to come back to this 'evil planet'.

What I understand more and more from my own experience and from others, is that Heaven is the ocean. It is always there. It is always around us. But we didn't see it, because we were too busy playing the Phase 1 game. Because it is always here we don't have to go anywhere. We can make the decision right now to live a lighter life by living from our center and in connection with our Higher Self. We can make the decision of already starting to remember our connection with Heaven right now. Or we can choose to look at life as Hell, when we choose to immerse ourselves completely into the Phase 1 game. On the planet of free will everybody can choose which game to play.

When you have made the decision to live your life in another way, to live life from your center in connection with your Higher Self, a new level of what I've written about in this book appears.

In this Chapter I will share how the Invitations from Chapter 2, the Ways from Chapter 4 and the Law of Attraction from Chapter 5 will change once you have decided to step up and commit to Phase 3 living.

Key 1: Alignment first, action second

Although I've pointed this important key out before, this is a good place to repeat it.

What 'alignment first, action second' means is to always be in your center before taking action. It is about BE-ing first and only DO-ing afterwards.

We saw in Chapter 5 that we can use our emotions as our guiding mechanism. The more we move towards the top of the scale, the better aligned we are with our Higher Self. As a result we are more in touch with the joyful state our Higher Self is in and the more effortlessly everything will go in our lives. The more towards the bottom of the scale, the less aligned we are.

So you can start using the scale to get closer to your Higher Self, by paying attention to how you feel. Look for ways to find relief. To find the resistance there is to move up the scale. Use for example, the Focus Wheel exercise.

The good news is that you don't have to get to the top of the scale to be in touch with your Higher Self. You are always in touch with It. It always guides you to more alignment.

Another easy way to deal with this, is to ask your Higher Self questions like:

- "What would feel better?"
- "What if this would be easy?"
- "What do you want me to do?"

Ask the question, and then wait for the answer. It can come immediately or take some time. This works differently from person to person, and case to case. Also remember that not everybody will perceive the response in the same way. Some will hear something or get an idea; others will see or feel the answer. So it's up to you to discover how you perceive answers. Don't fall in the trap of comparing yourself with others. Don't judge yourself because you can't feel the connection with your Higher Self as well as someone else can. Just relax and enjoy the experience as it unfolds.

Some people prefer to use tools or techniques in this process until they're confident in how they perceive information and answers. Although you don't need tools or techniques, they may help you in the beginning. People who have a harder time getting in touch with their feelings (or at least think they do ☺) or who don't trust their feelings enough yet, often find a tool or technique helps them feel more comfortable.

Some of the tools or techniques that are used:
- A pendulum
- (Tarot) Cards
- Kinesiology

Using these tools until you learn to trust your feelings can be helpful. You can also use them to bypass the wicked warriors as well. In other words: these tools can help you avoid the internal kicking and screaming your outpost can generate

Not everyone is prepared to work with external tools. If you want to work with one of them you need to let go of a preferred result as it can affect the outcome of the tool. For example, if you need to choose between two books and you prefer one book over another for some reason, working with a pendulum or kinesiologic tests won't help you pick the best option. If you test what book would be the best for you and you do that test a few times, your results may be different. Or the test may not work at all. The reason for the different results is the influence your preference is having. That's actually not a bad thing. Because you already know your preference, you don't need a tool or technique.

So in order to be able to test properly, you are invited to give up your attachment to the outcome. That is actually a very important key to live a center-based life in connection with your Higher Self as well. Whether or not you are going to use extra tools or techniques learn to detach from the outcome.

To sum up the insights from this first key:

- It is about alignment first, action second.
- Ask your Higher Self questions and wait for the response.
- If needed, use a tool or technique to help you. On the website you may find someone in the Directory who can teach you those tools or techniques.
- Give up attachment to the results or outcome.

Key 2: Let your Higher Self guide you

In the previous key you learned that giving up attachment to results is an important part of living from your center in conscious connection with your Higher Self.

Actually, the way to live an effortless and joyful life altogether is to give up attachment to everything. Now, don't get me wrong. It's not about living in poverty (although you may choose that route if you feel a strong desire to do that). It is living without attachment to a specific house, car, job, or relationship... You will probably still have all those things, but you won't feel attached to them anymore. When you are not attached to them, there is nothing to protect and nothing to lose, therefore there is nothing to defend or stress over. Isn't that a relaxing thought?

Actually, this is an excellent moment for you to also give up thinking that you know anything about life at all. It's a good time to give up believing that you are so smart you know the answers to all problems (oh yes, I know this last one all too well ☺). Since your Higher Self has a helicopter view, why not give it more control? Since your wicked warriors only have access to a collection of past experiences, your library of the past, and not to new opportunities, why not give up this way of living? Why not give up thinking that you, in your Human Form, are in the best position to draw the outline of your life? Since we are an extension of our Higher Self, it would serve our Higher Self to make the best decisions for us because It also benefits from it. I know this is a very daring suggestion and I don't expect you to go for it. To be honest, I'm also rather in the early stages of doing this myself. However during the times I was able to do so, my experiences have always been delightful.

If you are prepared to start playing with this key, start with the sentences I suggested before:

- "What would feel better?"
- "What if this would be easy?"
- "What do you want me to do?"

Ask your Higher Self the question in your mind or say it aloud. And then wait for the answer. Be aware that the answer may come in different ways. You may suddenly 'know' it, you may feel colder or warmer, you may suddenly get an idea (it may pop up in your mind or you may hear some kind of voice say it), you may receive an image or a kind of vision.

The way we get the answers to our questions differs from person to person. No two lives are the same. So please, don't start comparing experiences either. Avoid the so-called pitfall of the 'spiritual ego'. This is the fear-based ego of Phase 1 that has disguised itself as being 'very spiritual', but is in fact still acting from an attack/defense energy. It is still looking for acceptance and rejection, although it may seem it is not. I can testify from my own experience this disguise is one of the hardest to see ☺.

How to find out that the spiritual ego is at play?

For example ask yourself following questions:

- How important is it to me that I'm being perceived as 'spiritual'?
- How do I react when people say something that goes against my spiritual beliefs? Do I defend my spiritual beliefs? Do I think my approach is better than another? Am I in my outpost? Or can I let it go (and react from my center)?
- What is the language I use when talking about spirituality? Are there still many war-like words in my spiritual vocabulary?
- Do I try to convince others that my way of looking at spirituality is the best or the one and only?
- Have I been honest about my answers to the above questions? ☺

Let's assume the spiritual ego is not at play and let's look at some examples of the questions you can ask your Higher Self.

When you need to choose from a menu or between several pairs of shoes or pants, ask the question: "**What would feel better**?" And then see/feel what comes.

When you are faced with a more difficult decision, ask the question: "**What if this would be easy**?"

For example, a few years ago I had to take a flight from Orlando to Miami. I had attended the conference of the National Speaker Association in Orlando, flying in from Belgium. I was going to Miami and the Florida Keys for some vacation time afterwards. Because the Orlando-Miami flight was a so-called domestic flight there were other rules than for international flights regarding luggage. When I was waiting at the gate, I suddenly heard a broadcast: "The flight to Miami is completely full. We will check everybody's hand luggage very carefully to make sure it fits our regulations. And everybody is asked to stow their hand luggage under their chairs since there is not enough room in the overhead compartments."

I was not very pleased to hear this because my hand luggage was larger than allowed and since I have longer legs, giving up the space underneath the seat before me, would result in an uncomfortable flight. So I went in silence for a few moments and asked, "What if this would be easy?" The answer came within seconds: "You will be able to board rather quickly so you will be able to put your hand luggage in an overhead compartment. When you are in line, just look the steward or stewardess straight in the eyes, in a confident way. Then everything will be OK." And that's what happened. My ticket class could board as third. So there was enough room in the overhead compartments. When the steward came, I looked straight in his eyes and he even didn't look at my hand luggage even though he had been checking the hand luggage of the people in front of me and behind me!

Some people asked me afterwards, "How could you look at the steward in a comfortable way, when you were worried before?" In short, the answer is that I wasn't attached to the result. I was prepared to have to pay extra or to have my hand luggage go inside the cargo space. And I was willing to have an uncomfortable seating position. I was looking forward to having a nice vacation in beautiful surroundings. So I was OK with the worst-case scenario on the one hand, and I refused to focus on what could go wrong on the other hand.

When you have played with letting go of all your personal thoughts, preferences and specific situations, like a menu in a restaurant or your luggage when boarding a full flight, it may be time for the next step. Ask this question in the morning:

"What do You want me to do?"

This is one of the most powerful questions you can ask when you are ready to take your life to the next level. Be silent and wait for the answer to come. Remember that your Higher Self has the helicopter view. Get ready to be inspired and live a joyful life full of sweet surprises!

Key 3: Create new identifications

In Chapter 1 we have reviewed the process of how we identify with roles, places, people, objects, etc.

Sometimes identification provides us with a drive to do things and behave in a certain way. For example, the role of a parent may lead to compassionate behavior and a drive to provide for their children's comfort before their own.

However, most of the time identification brings limitations with it. For example, the role of a parent may bring the idea that you have to sacrifice yourself for your children, that you can't do your hobbies anymore, and that you have to decrease your social life to accommodate them. When your identifications were experienced from the outpost, you may have felt limited and restricted, even though you knew that the basis of all life is limitless freedom.

I don't know about you, but for me all identifications with roles, places, people and objects have conflicted at one time or another with that basis of freedom. Not because anyone else did anything to me, but because I had created this in my mind. That was how the world works in Phase 1. Now it is time to also change this part. Because we are now in our center and consciously connected to our Higher Self, it is time to recreate our old identifications and create new ones. Actually, we already started with recreating our old identifications in Chapter 2. It may be easier now to repeat that exercise since you are now in your center.

Besides reviewing your old identifications, you may want to create new ones. While you're at it, why not aim high instantly? Because our Human Form is only a small part of our total Infinite Being, let's incorporate some of the characteristics of that larger Being into an identity. Let's create an identity where we see ourselves as unlimited beings versus limited ones.

So every time you are in another role or you identify with something else and you say: "This can't be done for that reason," switch to the 'unlimited role', and have fun with it. I call my unlimited identification 'Super Jan' ☺. No he doesn't have a cape and the letter 'S' on his chest, but he is a pretty cool dude nonetheless ☺.

How does this work?

For example, "This restaurant is too expensive, I don't want to spend so much money on food. But it looks good."

I ask: "How would Super Jan feel or think in this situation? What would he do?" And then the answers will come.

They can be:
- "This is going to be a wonderful experience, I'm glad I can spend my money on this!"
- "Oh, I remember a restaurant close by that also has good food and is more reasonably priced. That would provide an excellent experience as well!"
- "What is it exactly that I want to experience? A good time with friends. This can be created in ways other than eating in an expensive restaurant!"

Since Super Jan is unlimited, anything can happen. And since there are no limits from this identification, there are no blocks to connect with my Higher Self. It becomes a straight channel.

Do I do this all the time?

To be honest: no. Sometimes I'm in my outpost with the noisy wicked warriors. And then it's harder to get into contact with Super Jan. When I'm in Phase 1 I often experience a lack of constructive and joyful energy. The chasm between them is too wide then. In other cases I just don't think about doing it. It is still something rather new for me as well. It hasn't become a habit yet. But that's not a problem at all. Even with my 'limited identifications' I have a good life when living from my center. Even though I'm not there all the time, it's good fun to create such an unlimited identification. Life becomes even more lightly, easy and effortlessly. Life becomes even more a Joyful Game!

Key 4: Self-Love

One of the key aspects of living a Joyful Life, of playing the Joyful Game of Life is Self-Love.

Self-Love builds further upon the foundation we have built in Chapter 2. Self-Love is based upon these principles:

- Remember that you created this game yourself.
- Take responsibility for everything that happens in your life. Give up victimhood (and remember that there is no one out there that is coming to get you).
- Forgive the world, embrace it and release it from your judgment towards it. Appreciate it for what it is: the neutral game board that allows you to play the games you want.
- Be aware of what you identify with (mind your words: which affirmations do you use? What do you say after "I AM …"?)
- Look at all your monsters, embrace them and turn them into teddy bears.
- Be totally honest about your monsters.
- Put yourself first (and remember that choosing for yourself is not choosing against someone).
- Be vulnerable so you become invulnerable.
- Be grateful for the roles other people play and have played.
- Forgive yourself for playing the Phase 1 game and choose to play the love-based game.
- Enjoy the game that you have created.

Self-Love is about living these principles on a daily basis. It is about a determined decision to choose to live your life in this way, and not from the outpost. It is about taking your power back and using it to create an extraordinary experience on planet Earth.

Those creations you make could be small ones, like making a delicious smoothie for your partner and yourself, or big ones like setting up an organization to connect people worldwide. Those creations will come from an inspired, fearless and unlimited Source. It's not about rescuing anyone anymore. It's about doing things that make your heart sing, things that are fun and that give you joy.

Self-Love is about relentlessly putting yourself in first place. From that spot you can be of assistance to other people. From that spot you can be an inspiration to other people, who may (or not) follow your example to exchange playing the Phase 1 game for playing the love-based game from their center, in conscious connection with their Higher Self.

And boy, what a joy it would be when more and more people begin to do this. We would all be uplifted more than ever before. Every time we had the slightest doubt and wanted to return to the Phase 1 game, others who were in their center would inspire us and immediately we would be back on track.

The good news is that we don't have to wait till everybody does this. Only a small percentage of people who live this way are enough to inspire the rest. Are you willing to be one of them? Are you willing to choose for yourself? Are you willing to be egoistic enough to only focus on Self-Love and in that way inspire others to do the same?

Key 5: Law of Attraction on another level

In the previous chapter we explored the process of attracting what you want, deliberately using the Law of Attraction. One of the questions was about not feeling passion (anymore) for worldly things like a car, a house, money, a relationship, a job, etc.

If you're not feeling passion anymore, not because you are overwhelmed or in a depression, it may be that it is time for you to REALLY start living differently. Chances are that it is an invitation to live from your center in conscious connection with your Higher Self and actually in connection with everything else. In other words: you're not experiencing an existence where separation is the primary way of looking at things. Instead you're seeing Oneness and Connectedness.

If you are at this level, the Law of Attraction still works - it is a Law, so it always works, whether you like it or not ☺. But, it works in a different way. When you are centered, when you are (sometimes or most of the time) connected, you can take the process of the Law of Attraction to a next level.

So let's look at what this may look like.

In short these are the 5 steps, inspired by the insights shared in the *Way of Mastery*:

1. Desire
2. Intention
3. The Answer Is Given
4. Allow
5. Surrender

Let's look at them one by one.

Desire

Your desire changes. It's not so much about material things anymore (although they are still part of your life). It's not so much about 'worldly things or status' anymore.

What is it about then?

It's a desire to be more connected. It's a desire to release the feeling of being separated and to welcome the feeling of Oneness, of Connectedness. It's a desire to feel the energy of Love more. It's a desire to be surrounded and immersed by that Love energy we've been talking about. It's a desire to feel the energy of Love flow through you. It's a desire to be able to radiate the energy of Love, to be the conduit of Love, to be the extension of Love.

It's a desire to be all your Higher Self, or God, the Universe, or what Spirit wants you to be, even if you don't have a clue as to what that may be. It's a desire to not have to think and worry about everything in your life, but a desire to be inspired. It's a desire to be carried by an energy that is bigger and larger than yourself. Although the desire becomes of a bigger dimension than before, the question actually gets simpler.

"What would You like me to do today?"

Although it sounds like giving up your own free choice to be an obedient slave to some kind of higher energy, like someone who doesn't ask questions and just follows orders, it is not like that at all.

I assume you have had some ideas in the past. Perhaps you were inspired in the past and you choose to take action or not. When you were really inspired and felt good about it, that inspiration gave you energy. Sometimes you even had enough energy to work long days with just a little bit of sleep. During those times you didn't even notice you were working so much, because you were *in flow*. Work didn't feel like work, it felt like play. It *gave* you energy instead of *draining* your energy.

I also assume that you liked this kind of experience and that you'd actually like to have more of it. Well, that is what this is about. It is about recognizing that that inspiration in the past came from your Higher Self. By asking, "What would You want me to do today?" you are actually asking for more inspiration so you can enjoy more flow moments that give you energy and joy!

Intention

Intention is about the willingness to choose the love-based game. It is about the commitment of going down this path instead of playing the Phase 1 game.

When you make the analogy with a laser sharp focus, desire is the laser and intention the mechanism that holds the laser in place.

Another important fact regarding intention is that when you notice yourself going back to playing the Phase 1 game, that you be mild and gentle with yourself. Instead of being mad, angry or frustrated with yourself, try saying: "Oh wow, I just played the Phase 1 game again. How interesting that I was distracted again. Now I choose to play the love-based game again."

The Answer Is Given

Like the process in Chapter 5, this is the step where your Higher Self gathers everything for you. You don't have to do anything.

Allow

Like we saw before in Chapter 5, *allowing* something to happen is different than *striving* for something. It's about being at the same vibrational level as what we desire.

It's also about trusting that the right events, places, people and objects will appear to provide us with what we want. Because we want different things when we are in our center and are consciously connected with our Higher Self than when we are not, other things will appear.

When we want less separation and more connectedness, things will happen in our life to show us where there are still parts of the Phase 1 game, the game of separation. New monsters will appear. However, we are now prepared to deal with them, because of the knowledge of the previous chapters of the book. Therefore it will be easier to transform our monsters into teddy bears.

Allowing is also 'admitting' that in our Human Form we don't know much. We admit we don't have the helicopter view, that we don't know what the best route is, that we don't know what will bring us the most joy. It is about acknowledging that our Higher Self is in a better position to see this and guide us towards it.

Surrender

The next step after allowing is surrendering.

Surrendering means not only 'admitting' that we don't know much in our Human Form, and that our Higher Self is in a better position to make those decisions, but also trusting Its guidance.

194

It is about trusting that our Higher Self knows the best way to experience—together with our Human Form— a Joyful Life. It is about trusting that It knows the best way to heal separation and to create oneness. It is about trusting that It will show us the ways to keep playing the love-based game. And that it will guide us back when we were distracted and fell into the Phase 1 game again.

However, humility is the key here. Not the worldly kind of humility, which is a fake kind of humility: "Although I love being applauded for what I did, I will say that it didn't mean much." Genuine humility is about understanding that the ideas were not made by you, in your Human Form. It is about knowing that it is your Higher Self that is providing you with insights, concepts, ideas, encounters and events. Inextricably connected to humility, is gratitude for this process: appreciation for the fact that you, in your Human Form, don't have to do it alone.

Humility and **appreciation** keep you in alignment with your Higher Self and in the vibration where you may receive what you have asked for. So keep putting these mindsets in practice. In the beginning it is particularly easy to forget about them, and as a consequence slide back in the Phase 1 game.

Just as the other steps about surrendering contain the decision to be centered instead of being in the outpost, humility and appreciation are just a decision. It is as easy as turning your head from left to right. It requires minimal effort. But it's YOU that needs to do it. I cannot do it for you, nor can anybody else. Not any guru, angel or saint, nor your husband, children, boss, colleague or employees can do this for you. It is up to you to make and implement the decision.

When you make the decision, and keep following the 5 steps you will be inspired. From a place of BE-ing you can start DO-ing. And it won't be just any kind of action. No, it will be *inspired action*, full of energy in which everything flows effortlessly. It will be a delight. And you will find yourself enjoying the Joyful Game of Life tremendously, just because you have taken the decision to do so, and because you are more than worth it!

Key 6: Be a Creator

As we saw before, our Human Form is a part of our larger Infinite Being. It is a form in which we can experience and create things that we cannot create in a non-physical form.

We are experiencing and creating our lives the whole time, but most of us are used to doing this in an unconscious way and inside the Phase 1 game.

So now it is time to change this. It is time to not only be conscious creators but conscious creators in the love-based game. With the foundation we have laid in the previous keys in this chapter we can now do things differently.

The best thing of all is: we don't have to do it alone. Our Higher Self will inspire and guide us. Action becomes Inspired Action. It becomes effortless action. We are carried along by our Higher Selves. So follow that inspiration. Follow your heart. Follow your intuition. Follow Joy.

Don't try to make things up yourself with your mind. Be inspired first and then allow your mind and body to execute the inspiration. Don't follow the mind and body that are led by the wicked warriors. Reverse the roles and enjoy the ride.

Go from survive to *live*. Create what you are inspired to do. Don't make it overcomplicated. Creating can mean building a house, inventing a new product or setting up an organization. But it also can mean making a sandwich, drawing a picture, organizing a party, writing a letter, baking a cake, etc. Just feel what gives you joy and follow that feeling. Act on that inspiration.

Be a creator!

Key 7: Use every moment to extend Love

When you have made the decision to play the love-based game instead of the Phase 1 game, there is one simple, though profound thing you can do.

You can use every moment to extend Love.

What do I mean by that?

Use every moment (or to start with: the moments when you think of it ☺) to communicate from your connected center. Use every moment to be in your connected center and respond and act from there to allow anything that happens. Do this, even in rather scary moments. For example, when you find yourself in a discussion with someone who is clearly acting from his or her outpost.

What I do when I'm in such a situation and don't know what to do or say, is go into my center first and then ask: "What do You want me to say?" When I'm in my center (and whether or not I'm aware of my connection with my Higher Self) and when I focus on only wanting to radiate Love, there always comes some kind of inspiration of what to say that will (gradually) calm down the situation.

Something else that I do when I find myself in a situation with someone who is angry, mad or frustrated, is go to my center and say inside my mind and heart: "The I AM presence in me sees the I AM presence in you." This is another way of saying that I acknowledge there is something bigger than me (of which my Human Form and my Higher Self are part of) that is only Love and that both the other person and I are part of. In this way I invite the other person on a vibrational level to leave their outpost and go to their center.

Extending Love in these ways has a double advantage, one, I can assist the other person and two; I'm already experiencing what I'm wanting. To extend Love is to experience Love. Isn't it great how that works?

These examples are just two of the things I do. Do you see how easy it can be? I invite you to start doing this yourself. Create your own simple ways of extending Love. Just do it for yourself. Because you will feel love at the same time, it is the most egoistic and altruistic thing you can do at one time!

How to consciously connect?

After reading through the keys of Chapter 6 you may wonder: "I would love to experience this, but how do I get consciously connected with my Higher Self?"

Well, the tips from Chapter 4 will help you to get more into your center. But maybe you have done some of the exercises or processes and have already experienced some kind of connection with your Higher Self. So you know it works the same way. In other words: use the tips from Chapter 4 to not only get into your center, but also to get consciously connected with your Higher Self.

Other ways to experience the connection more is to look at the tips, tools, exercises and techniques from Chapter 2 and 3 from another point of view. If you look at them from your center you will discover deeper levels. At least that's what happened to me ☺. So look at those chapters again and play with them!

Chapter 7: Life Cycle, Relationships, Money and Health

This book is just the beginning ☺.

There are lots of topics that haven't been covered in here, such as:

- Relationships:
  - Relationship between partners: how can you experience the love-based game together?
  - Relationship with children: how to introduce your children to the game and play the human game together in harmony?
  - Working together professionally: what to keep in mind?
  - Attraction between people: what happens at the beginning of our relationships, and then what happens next?
- Life cycle
  - What do we bring to this planet when we are born?
  - The energetic patterns of marriage
  - What happens when passing over (dying)?
- Attracting the right people
  - Life Partner
  - Business Partner(s)
  - Customers
  - Employees
  - Investors
- Money
  - What is money, the abundance or the lack of it, really about?
  - How to let money flow better in our lives (more income, right outflow)
- Body
  - What is the role of the body?
  - Why is there disease?
  - What is the role of sex?
  - How to make love from a love-based game perspective?

The answers to those questions will be covered in articles, videos, webinars, workshops, seminars and additional books. So keep an eye on the website and make sure you create a free account so you'll have access to all this extra content and so you can be notified when new content becomes available!

Last words

If you read this book in one sitting, you may feel overwhelmed. If you are still in Phase 1 energy, there probably will be lots of parts in the book that you feel resistance, or even anger about.

If you were reading this, being centered most of the time, but not in conscious connection with your Higher Self yet, you may find yourself in a weird place. At least I was when I was in this part of my awakening process. I was feeling tossed between two 'worlds'; the world of the fear-based game and the world of the love-based game. That period in time was sometimes difficult: I had chosen to pursue the love-based game, but was thrown back many times into Phase 1. At those moments it was hard to believe the love-based game could be the way to go, especially when listening to the radio and watching television where fear-based energy still reigns. But even if I'm not consciously connected the whole time, I can already say, it's good to live 'on the other side' ☺. My life has become so much more peaceful, calm, quiet and effortless. I wish this for everybody!

As I mentioned, you may feel overwhelmed: "Wow, I still have so much work to do." You may even be triggered (as I was when starting my own process). You may find yourself saying, "I'm not good enough, I'm not powerful enough, I'm never going to be able to do this. Where do I start?"

I have good news for you! You don't have to DO anything! If you are reading this page, the most important part already happened: you read the entire book. The shift from Phase 1 living to centered living has already started. Your awareness is already shifting. You are already more conscious (and hence already a bit more en-light-ened than before). Maybe you even have already experienced some visible changes in your daily life!

Now it is up to you. You can read the book again. Or put it away for a while and do nothing else. Or read it again in a few years. Or take a next step. It's all up to you. Nothing else really NEEDS to be done. Remember that everybody's path is different. Just because your book club read this book and some members are wildly enthused to take a next step, doesn't mean you have to join them. Follow your feelings and make a decision from your centered spot, not when you are in close contact with the fear-based energy.

If you feel inspired to take a next step, go back to the part of the book you felt enthusiastic about or that touched you in any way (probably even in a way that you can't explain). Look at what it was and then go to the website to find more information about it whether it's in a video, a blog article, a reference to a person or a website, or when it is about a specific method or technique. Search in the Directory of coaches, healers, facilitators and therapists someone near to you that specializes in the topic you feel connected to.

If you feel that I can help you, as a fellow student, to gain more insights or if you feel that you can learn from my experiences, check out the calendar with public workshops and seminars or attend a webinar or an online course.

I hope that you have realized throughout this book that I'm also still on my way to getting lighter and lighter. I too am still facing fears and transforming monsters into teddy bears on a daily basis. In other words, I won't be able to save you (nor do I choose to make any attempt at this ☺), but I can continue to offer you more insights from what I have learned on my path. So if you want to play according to this 'rule', then I sincerely look forward to having a heart-to-heart encounter with you!

With much Love !

Jan

Words of Gratitude

I'm very grateful for the people who have played their roles in my life. Whether they took on the role of adversary, ally or resource, they all have contributed to my fantastic Game of Life so far.

I would like to explicitly express my gratitude for the people who played a role in the game of writing this book:

- Gwendolyn for standing besides me, being a source of inspiration and being my main buddy in facing the monsters and turning them into teddy bears.
- My mother Mia, father Ivo, brother Bert and sister-in-law Vickie for their loving support.
- Becky Blanton, Phil Elmore and Annemie Janssens for the great editing work.
- Wim Van Acker, Inge Dom, Deirdre Morris, Samuel Bosch, Nick Limère, Paul Meert, Wouter Murrath, Maria Verduijn, Tania Dewinne and Nienke Van Oeveren for their much appreciated feedback.
- Priscilla Peeters for the great artwork.
- And the team at Graffito for the inspiring cover.

About the Author

Hi, my name is Jan Vermeiren. I'm the founder of 'Life is a Game!' This organization is focused on assisting people to live a lighter life via personal and spiritual growth programs.

In my life before 'Life is a Game' I was the founder of Networking Coach (which merged in 2014 with Really Connect). I wrote two books, *Let's Connect* and *How to REALLY use LinkedIn*.

Until now the company has been working for more than 450 companies and organizations worldwide. We were the first LinkedIn training partner on planet Earth. So you could say that I was pretty successful ☺.

However, something was missing. I felt that I had touched upon the essence of Life now and again, but I always lost the connection. Now I understand that I was being pulled back into the Phase 1 game. This motion was felt in my work and in the company. Although both books and all the training programs at Networking Coach were based on universal or spiritual principles, the focus was more on practical insights and technological tips about how to be successful in Phase 1 of the human game.

With 'Life is a Game!' I officially go to the next "level" in my human game. After having played for some time in Phase 2 and having experienced life in Phase 3 once in a while, I'm now ready to assist others in doing the same: living a lighter, more peaceful, and especially much more joyful life!

If you want to play along, you can find more tips, insights, articles, videos and exercises on **www.life-is-a-game.org** .

Next steps

Maybe there are no next steps for you ☺. Maybe the content of this book was enough for you, at least for a while.

Remember that there is much more background information, examples, videos and articles about topics that haven't been covered in the book. You can find them in the free Library on the website **www.life-is-a-game.org**.

I'm also planning to do more webinars about the individual topics in the book, so look at the calendar or register for these webinars in the Library. Then you will automatically receive notifications of a variety of upcoming events where you can ask your own questions.

If you would like personal support and information for your specific circumstances, visit the directory of coaches, therapists, healers and facilitators on the website.

For seminars, workshops and events where I am the speaker, or that we organize ourselves: look at the calendar on the website.

If your organization wants to hire me as a speaker or wants to organize a workshop, feel free to contact our office at: **connect@life-is-a-game.org**.

www.ingramcontent.com/pod-product-compliance
Lightning Source LLC
Chambersburg PA
CBHW062041090426
42740CB00016B/2978